GHOSTS AND SPIRITS:
INSIGHTS FROM A
MEDIUM

ROB GUTRO

The cover photo is one that I took in 1993 using a Canon 35 mm camera. There was no flash used because there was enough natural light from a window that was located to the right side while facing the painting. It is a painting that hangs in the lobby of Tombstone, Arizona's Bird Cage Theatre. The woman in the painting is a famous actress of the late 1800s named Fatima. If you look closely at the lower portion of the painting, you'll see the ghostly face of the old man that haunts the Bird Cage Theatre. I was as surprised when the former manager of the Bird Cage called to tell me after receiving a copy of the photo from me. I was told that this ghost may have been one of the actors that performed in the theatre and simply never left. He's also been spotted on the stage of the theatre.

The individual experiences in this book are true. However, in some instances, full names have been altered or abbreviated at the request of the person or persons providing the story, to protect their privacy.

"Ghosts and Spirits: Insights From a Medium," by Rob Gutro. ISBN 978-1-60264-513-4 (softcover); 978-1-60264-514-1 (ebook).

Manufactured in the United States of America.

December 2013

Mary · Joe

I hope this book
brings you comfort
and makes you aware
of how Nick is giving you
messages — He wants you
to be in good spirits because
his love surrounds you.

DEDICATION

This book is dedicated to Tom and to our dogs Dolly, Franklin, and the
late puppy Buzz Wyatt. All of them taught me the meaning of
unconditional love and provided support and inspiration to write this
book. It was only through the power of love that I was able to enhance
my abilities to communicate with spirits, either Earth-bound or those
who have passed, and understand the why and how of their messages.

CONTENTS

FOREWORD

I consider myself an average middle-aged guy. I'm a scientist and scientific writer by trade, but since I was a teenager I've had the ability to see, sense and communicate with ghosts and Earth-bound spirits.

For decades I haven't paid much attention to my abilities, because I didn't understand them, and I wasn't spiritually or emotionally mature enough to do so. Years ago I fell in love and now I'm happily married. Since I met my partner, my abilities increased a hundred-fold. That was when I decided to learn much more about those who have passed, those who have crossed over into the light (spirits) and those who remain Earth-bound (ghosts). I've discovered a lot of information that clarified questions I've had and I've written this book to share it with you.

There is a difference between Earth-bound ghosts and spirits, and the methods they utilize to communicate with the living. It's important to maintain an open mind to things we don't understand. Our souls are living energy, and we are all connected while we are alive and even after we pass.

This book will help explain who, what, where, when, why, and the difference between ghosts and spirits. There are a lot of books out there on the topic, but not one that I've found that distinguishes between the two entities.

I've had a lot of personal experiences and have shared them in this book to help you understand how ghosts and spirits communicate with the living.

I feel blessed that I can receive these messages from those who have passed, and have been grateful to help others better cope with their losses. In my own life, my abilities have helped both my partner Tom and me, and some friends cope with the losses of family members and pets. Although I am still in what I consider the "early stages" of being able to communicate with spirits and Earth-bound ghosts, I continue to refine my abilities and try to assist people with messages from the beyond.

I hope this book will provide you as a reader with a better understanding of the difference between Earth-bound ghosts and spirits who have passed into the light, and the methods they utilize to communicate with the living. It's important to maintain an open mind to things we don't understand. Our souls are living energy, and we are all connected while we are alive and even after we pass.

I would like to thank those who believe in my ability. A special thank you to our friend Jane, who so willingly volunteered to provide edits on this book.

I'm not a medium that makes appointments or charges people for readings, because I'm still learning how to refine my abilities. There are a number of mediums that you can contact if you'd like personal readings and you can find them using the Internet. I'm still working my way up to that stage in my level of ability.

If you have questions or stories you'd like to share please feel free to write me at Rgutro@gmail.com, or write on my blog: *http://ghostsandspiritsinsights.blogspot.com.*

I look forward to hearing from you.

INTRODUCTION

Ghosts and spirits. From a young age, I've known of their existence. I consider myself an average, middle-aged guy. I'm also a meteorologist, so the scientist in me wants to prove they exist. I have. I have also learned the difference between a ghost and a spirit and this book explains that to you.

I've sensed them, seen them, felt them, and heard them. I didn't ask for this ability; but have come to realize it's inherited and it's a gift. My ability has grown as I've grown older and my emotional state has been heightened. I'm no longer afraid of them. I've found that being afraid of spirits prevents them from coming to you; however, they may come to someone else as they can be persistent in getting their messages across.

There's something unique about this world where emotion and science come together in the form of energies we call ghosts and spirits. And there's a difference between the two. In this book, I'll define the difference and share stories of my encounters and encounters others have had in sight, sound and feel with these beings of energy.

A part of this book includes stories submitted by friends, family, or acquaintances that I have known for some time. All of these accounts are true. They hold special memories in the minds and hearts of those willing to share them. In doing so, he intent is that others may read and come to believe that there's more to this world than meets the eye.

I believe that God grants people, and animals, the ability to return to Earth; these are spirits. Once they pass into the light, spirits have the ability to return to those they loved for short periods of time to give them messages.

Ghosts differ from spirits in that they remain on Earth. Ghosts stay Earth-bound for many reasons that include: a sudden or violent death, they don't seem to understand they've passed on, they want revenge, they seek forgiveness for something they did in life, or they may have unfinished business. This book will explain what I've learned about ghosts and spirits from personal encounters and from various other sources. I hope that this book gives you insight and provide a better understanding of the spirit world.

CHAPTER 1
Growing Up and Developing an Understanding

I grew up hearing about spirits and ghosts. My first introduction to them was in church where I heard about the Holy Spirit or Holy Ghost. This exposed me to the concept of a being of "energy" or "light" (light is energy after all). My first encounter with ghosts or spirits of people happened when I was 16 years old and my grandfather's spirit appeared to me, months after his passing.

My beliefs about the afterlife came from attending the Catholic Church in my hometown in Massachusetts. My parents sent us to "Sunday school" which was curiously held on Wednesday afternoons after school.

There's a big difference between "ghosts" and "spirits." Spirits have transitioned to the next plane of existence, what we would think of as "Heaven." Ghosts, however, have not left the Earth.

Ghosts and spirits are made up of energy. Like an energy of a person or animal's soul. I believe that love is also an energy (a positive one) between two living beings, human or animal, or something each species has for the other, such as a dog and its master. On the flip side of that, it's easy to see that hatred and fear are negative energies. I'll discuss how those energies cause ghosts or spirits to manifest themselves later.

God, angels, saints, and spirits are all about energy. God is love, and love is positive energy. I believe that love and its energy is inside each and every one of us, and its up to use to express it. Dogs and cats are living embodiments of unconditional love. They, like people, have spirit energy, and they pass like people do. Anyone who says dogs and cats don't have souls or spirits is simply uninformed. Our pets are waiting for us on the other side when it's our time to pass. I've seen them on the other side, as have many, many mediums.

If people would only learn from their pets, the world would be a better place. Animals show unconditional love, and I have experienced that their energy (and love) are always around their masters. There is a section later in this book with examples of how pets who have passed on have given signs to their masters, that they come back and visit their loved ones and the love lives on.

Love isn't religion. Religions are conceived by man. I do believe that religions offer a good guideline for people to understand god, develop faith for use in many aspects of their lives and treat others as they would expect to be treated. If people actually loved as they're instructed through their religions, we'd have fewer wars, and less people killing, cheating or hurting others. Those people, however, will see all of their wrongdoings when they pass from this life to the next and will have to account for their bad behavior. It is some of those people who chose not to pass into the light for fear of being judged on their earthly doings, who remain Earth-bound ghosts.

The bottom line is that religions are a good base in which to develop a faith in a higher power. Religion, however, has become too political and many churches now have agendas that are not teaching "love and acceptance all people," despite what they may say up front. After 40 years of Catholicism, I finally realized this and no longer support organized religions that have political agendas (i.e., most of them). We are all part of the energy that is God. We are all connected with each other. We all have God's love and energy and that love and energy should be shared with everyone. No one is any better or worse than another.

CHAPTER 2
What is a Ghost and What Enables Them to Appear?

Ghosts and spirits are energy from a life that previously existed. We know that the universe is made up of matter and energy, and energy is everywhere. Energy is the conduit in which ghosts and spirits are able to manifest themselves. Ghosts and spirits use different kinds of energy to make themselves known. This chapter discusses types of energy that ghosts and spirits use to manifest themselves to the living.

Electricity provides a means that enables spirits to manifest themselves. If you think about stories you've heard where ghosts haunt places, electrical things are often affected. Lights and batteries are often turned on or off, or batteries are drained when a ghost wants to manifest itself. That's because ghosts/spirits are energy and when they want to do something such as move an object, or be seen, they need to draw on energy, such as electricity, or emotional energy. Despite what our culture has taught us, cemeteries aren't really haunted. At least they aren't populated with ghosts, until a living person goes to one and supplies emotional energy for a ghost to draw energy from. Think of a ghost or spirit as a "low battery" and that gets "recharged" when there's new energy, such as electricity, emotion, water or heat to "power them back up."

Emotional energy works in the same manner as electricity. Think of a group of people who are excited about something. They give off "energy," whether positive or negative. Negative energy is what Earth-bound ghosts thrive on and use to manifest themselves. Negative emotions, such as overwhelming grief experienced after a loved one has passed, can actually block a person's senses to a spirit who is trying to come through to them. Positive emotions, such as optimism and happiness, seem to enable a spirit (one who passed into the light) to come back and provide messages to a living loved one.

Moving Water is another kind of energy in nature that ghosts and spirits use to manifest themselves. If there's a river through a town, as in old Ellicott City, Maryland, you'll find a lot of hauntings. Water power is not limited to rivers, though. Ghosts or spirits can use water of any kind, including a shower, as long as the water is moving. Motion equals energy. I had one instance in which this happened to me. James Van Praagh, a famous medium, recommends putting out a bowl of water to assist a spirit when you're trying to make contact, but I recommend running water out of a tap.

Heat is another kind of energy that ghosts utilize to make themselves known. When you think about the physics of heat, it's created when matter (made up of atoms and molecules, which are groupings of atoms) and energy cause the atoms and molecules to always be in motion - either bumping into each other or vibrating back and forth. That motion of atoms and molecules creates a form of energy called "heat" or thermal energy, which is present in all matter. Even in the coldest void of space, matter still has a very small but measurable amount of heat energy.

In order to "energize themselves" and appear, ghosts and spirits absorb heat energy, which basically slows down the movement of the molecules. Science dictates that would create a cooling effect, producing a "cold spot" from which the energy has been removed from the moving molecules. That's why ghosts are associated with "cold spots." Those cold spots are areas where a ghost or spirit is present and trying to manifest itself.

Think of how a hurricane needs warmer ocean waters to get stronger. A spirit is the same way. They need warmer temperatures (with fast moving molecules) to come together. What happens when they slow down the molecules and become visible or are able to make themselves known through other ways is that the air becomes cooler. Molecules in cold air move much slower than those in warm air.

CHAPTER 3
Two Kinds of Ghosts/Spirits

Now that we know that ghosts and spirits are energy-beings and we can basically say that a "soul" is energy, we need to know that there are two kinds of them. There are Earth-bound ghosts and there are spirits who have passed into "the light." I'll define "the light" shortly.

There's a big difference between these two entities. Earth-bound ghosts are the ones that haunt places. They chose not to pass into "the light" and onto the next phase of life. Ghosts attach themselves to a place in which they're familiar or where they may have died tragically. Ghosts can also attach themselves to people and come home with them. If a person loved an object immensely when they were alive, sometimes they don't want to let it go after they pass; some of their energy can also be left on a physical object such as a piece of furniture.

Spirits, on the other hand, realized their life on Earth was over and they passed into the light to the next phase of life.

When people are about to pass, the spirits of pre-deceased family members will appear to them to help them cross over. There are countless stories of people on their death beds who see deceased relatives standing in the room. These spirits of late family members can take a person into the light on their death bed, after their wake or after their funeral. Many times, spirits of people who just pass will linger until their funeral is over to see who attended. Then they'll pass into the light. Such was the case with my own father, as I watched him pass into the light after his burial.

Spirits can come back from within the light to loved ones whenever they want to bring messages or whenever living loved ones talk to them. Spirits can also appear anywhere on Earth. They're not limited to the place in which they passed or bound to places they knew when alive. They usually come back to provide helpful messages to those they loved or knew when they were alive. They have the ability to appear to anyone, such as a medium, as long as they can get their message to the one they love left on Earth. Such was the case of my friends' mother and grandmother.

GHOSTS (EARTH BOUND)

Earth-bound ghosts are those souls that elect to stay behind for one reason or another. For example, if a person is killed suddenly, they may not realize they're dead and linger on Earth. Or, they may think they need to stay behind to help a grieving family get over their death. Or, they may be afraid of facing judgment in the light. Oftentimes, people who commit suicide choose to stay Earth-bound because they are scared of "going to hell" as they may have been falsely told by their religion. People who commit suicide do not go to hell.

Getting to the other side and into the light is about love and forgiveness: forgiving one's self as well as others.

Earth-bound ghosts can also stay around on Earth to obtain forgiveness for some bad things they did when they were alive. Such was the case of one of my own aunts, which I'll explain later as she, too, came to me. It is important that those who passed before us are forgiven, so they can pass into the light and not linger on Earth. Forgiveness is extremely important to Earth-bound ghosts.

TWO TYPES OF HAUNTINGS

There are two different kinds of ghosts and hauntings: "intelligent hauntings" and "residual hauntings."

During an intelligent haunting, ghosts have independent thought, and can do things, such as move objects, make noises or make appearances. These are things found in "haunted houses."

Another example, called an "apport" is explained later. Briefly, this happens when an object is moved by paranormal means. For example if your keys are misplaced, you check the area where you know you left them, and they're not there. When you come back later, they're mysteriously there, although there's no one else in the house. Footsteps are very common in intelligent haunts. These ghosts are Earth-bound and they need to be told to go to the "light" and pass onto the next plane of existence. There are also human and "dark" or non-human spirits. Non-human spirits are just "dark entities" that people have reported in haunted houses or other places. I've seen one dark entity, and I immediately sensed it was negative energy. It was, in fact, pretty scary.

Another way Earth-bound ghosts are seen is in "residual hauntings." Residual hauntings are like the after-glow of a camera flash. That is, when a traumatic event happens, energy is "left behind" and the event keeps running over and over as a visible image, just like a camera flash stays in your eyes after someone takes a photo of you. Residual haunts are not intelligent haunts. They can't interact with people, send people messages, or leave electronic voice phenomena. They always appear the same. Basically, it's like watching a movie replay in a loop, and that movie will never change.

Residual hauntings can also mean that a ghost's energy is attached to an object the person loved during his lifetime. One story from Ellicott City, Maryland, involved the sale of a rocking chair that belonged to his grandfather. After the grandfather passed, the chair was sold on commission to an antique store in the town. Someone bought it, and later returned it when they noticed the chair rocking by itself and then a transparent figure rocking in the chair. I've felt spirits attached to things. In fact, we had a mattress in our home that had a woman's energy attached to it.

POLTERGEISTS

Poltergeists have a reputation for being restless, angry, disturbed or unhappy ghosts. According to Wikipedia, the word "poltergeist" comes from the German word "poltern," meaning to rumble or make noise, and "geist," meaning "ghost." A poltergeist is a demonic ghost that manifests itself by moving and influencing objects and making loud noises. That definition is being disputed, however.

According to the Physics and Mediums Web site (*http://www.psychics.co.uk/*) from the United Kingdom, "Most paranormal researchers believe that poltergeists are not ghosts at all, but manifestations of unconscious mental upset, usually in children or teenagers." The website explains that objects are moved or noises are created as a result of a troubled teen's psychic energy. Moving an object with your mind is called "psychokinesis." The word comes from the word "psyche" meaning "mind" and "kinesis" meaning "motion."

Psychokinesis was first used by American author-publisher Henry Holt in his 1914 book called *On the Cosmic Relation*. It appeared again in 1934, from Holt's friend Joseph B. Rhine, who used the word in his experiments to see if a person could influence the roll of dice. Rhine was a parapsychologist who actually founded the parapsychology lab at Duke University, the *Journal of Parapsychology*, and the Foundation for Research on the Nature of Man at Duke University in Durham, North Carolina.

Anyone that has watched the popular ghost hunting television program, "Ghost Hunters" on the SyFy Channel, has encountered some of these instances. One case involved a teen girl who reported things moving around in her bedroom. When the Ghost Hunters, Jason and Grant, stayed in the room, nothing occurred. When the girl was brought back into the room, the equipment registered something. The young girl appeared to be the source of the "paranormal" activity.

Usually, the emotions associated with the poltergeist activity include anxiety, paranoia, schizophrenia and, of course, anger. Often, psychological counseling can help reduce the "poltergeist" activity by dealing with these issues.

SPIRITS

Spirits have passed into the "light" and onto the next phase of their lives. The "light" is considered heaven, where souls/spirits find peace, love and knowledge. By having passed into the light, spirits are able to manifest and communicate to the living in various locations, whereas ghosts are limited to the places they knew or objects owned when alive.

Spirits are in a good place and can watch over people on Earth and help, guide and protect them. Spirits can also manifest themselves, usually to their loved ones or to a medium who can detect them and communicate what they need to their loved one. Spirits communicate, but not as often as Earth-bound ghosts, who are trying to convey a message to get help. Spirits come back to help the living, while ghosts seek help from the living.

One way spirits communicate to us is through our dreams. If you dream of someone who has passed, then that means they've crossed into the light. Earth-bound ghosts cannot appear in dreams.

I've heard often that people who dream of loved ones who've passed away often see them in peaceful settings like a field or sitting on a porch swing talking and laughing. In 2008, my partner dreamed of his late partner walking with him and talking in a peaceful setting.

CHAPTER 4
Where do Ghosts and Spirits Appear?

Ghosts or Earth-bound entities are attached to things or places. Spirits can appear almost anywhere, any time and aren't governed by the laws of nature on Earth. As I mentioned previously, ghosts are trying to get help from the living, while spirits come back to help the living.

In ghost stories, an entity frequently haunts a house or location and stays there.

Despite what our culture has taught us in literature, cemeteries aren't really haunted. At least they aren't populated with ghosts until a living person goes to one and supplies emotional energy for a ghost to draw energy from. When you think about most hauntings, however, ghosts haunt places they were familiar with in life. Most people when alive are not familiar with, or attracted to cemeteries, so why would they haunt them (unless they were killed in them)?

Sometimes ghosts will use their energies to make something happen that shows their presence to the living. Making pennies or other objects appear (an apport), doors slam, or objects move, are examples of this.

According to the *Historical Terms Glossary of the Parapsychological Association*, "An apport is the paranormal transference of an article from one place to another or an appearance of an article from an unknown source."

David Fontana's, *Is There an Afterlife: A Comprehensive Review of the Evidence*, notes that "Apports are often associated with poltergeist activity, and on rare occasions are said to be witnessed landing on the floor, in a person's lap or dropping from the ceiling. Flowers are a well known form of apport at spiritualistic séances, but tar and mud have also been reported."

Chapter 12 describes actual experiences of pennies appearing and Chapter 17 flowers blooming mysteriously.

There is an opposite side to an apport: an "Asport." According to the Kentucky Paranormal Research group, an asport is the transference of a small object from a known location to an unknown location via paranormal means.

Ghosts can attach themselves to people and follow them back to their residence. It's important for people to rid themselves of any attached ghosts before they leave a haunted place. This is discussed more in Chapter 6.

Ghosts are usually found in places with many people. Ghosts and spirits feed off energy, emotional energy or heat or electric energy. You'll rarely find ghosts in a cemetery, because there are no sources of living energy to "power them."

Earth-bound ghosts tend to cling to things that are familiar or important to them. When a person is killed suddenly, the ghost may haunt the place they met their fate.

HAUNTING AN AREA OF SUDDEN DEATH

One morning in December, 2006, when I lived in Elkridge, Maryland, I drove by an island marker on Route 1 southbound that was at the end of an off-ramp from Route 100 onto Route 1 south. I sensed the ghost of an Hispanic man standing on the traffic island looking down and around. I immediately got the sense that he was recently killed there in an accident. When I got to work, I called my partner, Tom, who had left the house 2 hours earlier to go to work. He said that there was a pick-up truck that had flipped over onto the island, and the person was likely dead. He said at that hour the police and fire department were finishing cleaning up the scene, and a tow truck was there.

The next day when we drove by, there were flowers and a cross, indicating that someone had indeed died there. For the next couple of days, Tom kept checking the news, and it turned out that an Hispanic man from Glen Burnie, Maryland (about 15 minutes east of Elkridge) drove through a flashing red light at the end of the off-ramp from Route 100 onto Route 1. The man was killed.

When I drove by around 6:30 a.m., I had sensed that hours after his sudden death, the man's ghost was still lingering there, trying to understand that he had been killed.

Here's the official accident report from the Howard County, Maryland that Tom located:

NEWS RELEASE
HOWARD COUNTY DEPARTMENT OF POLICE
OFFICE OF PUBLIC AFFAIRS
For Release: Dec. 4, 2006 Contact: Sherry Llewellyn
PFC Jennifer Reidy
(410) 313-2236
Driver Killed After Failing to Stop For Flashing Red Light
The Howard County Police Department is investigating a fatal collision that occurred this morning that resulted in the death of a Glen

Burnie driver. The collision took place as the driver tried to merge onto Route 1, failed to stop at a flashing red light and was struck by a tractor trailer.

At approximately 4:50 a.m., a 2000 Chevrolet S10 pickup truck being driven by Israel Castaneda, 27, exited westbound Route 100 to continue onto southbound Route 1. The pickup entered the intersection, which is controlled by a flashing red light for those coming off the ramp, but failed to stop for the signal. Castaneda continued onto Route 1, where he was struck by a tractor trailer that was traveling north on Route 1. The pickup truck flipped over, killing the driver.

Based on the information available, investigators believe Castaneda to be at fault and do not anticipate pressing charges against the driver of the tractor trailer, who has been identified as Wallace Townson, 33, of Sykesville.

The investigation is continuing.

Source:

http://www.howardcountymd.gov/police/docs/fatal120406.pdf

Days later, Mr. Castenada's ghost was gone - which made sense to me. What happens in such cases is that a person who is suddenly killed, lingers until they realize they're dead. They sometimes find their way to their own funeral or wake where they tend to pass into the light. Otherwise, the can return to where they lived, realize they're dead and pass into the light there.

GHOSTS: COMING OR GOING

Usually, those who go to their own wake will pass into the light. I've read from authors and psychic mediums James Van Praagh and Mary Ann Winkowski, that people always attend their own services. It's a natural curiosity for people to want to see what they look like laid out in a funeral home and who shows up. If someone is cremated, the ghost will still go to the funeral home to see who came to pay respects. There doesn't have to be a physical body – just something that will draw the ghost there. In the case of people who were missing and never found, ghosts can find their way to gatherings in their honor.

So, next time you're at a wake or funeral and you think about saying something bad about the dead, think again, because they can certainly hear you.

After services end, the light usually appears in funeral homes, and the spirits walk into it. If you do encounter an Earth-bound ghost, you need to tell them to go into the light. Tell them to seek out a funeral home and pass through the light there. You can communicate with ghosts and spirits either by voicing your thoughts out loud, or simply by thinking them, because thoughts are made up of electrical energy, just as the ghosts and spirits are energy.

It has been my experience that ghosts seem to listen more when a person speaks out loud, rather than trying to communicate by thought, whereas spirits communicate entirely by thought from both the living person and the spirit.

Why do thoughts work as communication with ghosts and spirits? Thoughts are energy. Think of scientists and doctors that use Electroencephalography or EEG.

An EEG is a recording of electrical activity made along a person's scalp produced when neurons fire within the brain. In clinical terms, an EEG is a recording of the brain's spontaneous electrical activity over a short period of time between 20–40 minutes. Electrodes record EEGs when placed on the scalp.

Basically, thoughts are electrical impulses in the brain. Those impulses are created by neurons, or nerve cells. Neurons are electrically active cells which are primarily responsible for carrying out the brain's functions.

As for where Earth-bound ghosts are found, I've noticed that Earth-bound ghosts will typically choose to stay in surroundings they were comfortable in, or familiar with when they were alive. This is why many houses are haunted by their former residents.

However, ghosts can also inhabit the place where they died whether it is in a hospital, house or battlefield. In Chapter 15: Experiences in Various Houses and Locations, I describe my visit to an historic house in Maryland, where two children who died in the 1800s still walk in the house where they were raised.

Spirits, however, are not limited to any location. Because spirits have passed into the light, they have the ability to be anywhere in the world, even in different places at the same time.

Ghosts and positive or negative energies associated with them can also attach themselves to an object they loved when alive, such as a chair or other piece of furniture. They can also follow their ashes when placed in an urn and taken into a house.

KEEPING ASHES IN THE HOUSE ENABLES SPIRITS

I've found through personal experience that having an urn or other container with a person or pet's ashes enables a spirit or ghost to come into a house. At one time I lived with a roommate who brought an urn containing his late mother's ashes into my house. When my roommate's mother was alive, she had a number of emotional challenges and suffered from bipolar disorder and anger problems. My roommate told me she could be both kind and cruel and was abusive to him as he was growing up.

One night, while the ashes were in the house, both my roommate and I were awakened at the same time in the early morning hours when a dark shadowy figure appeared in the hallway between the bedroom doors. I believe it may have been my roommate's mother, although I couldn't be certain.

I prayed aloud that God would protect me and that it go away, and it did. I had never experienced a dark shadowy figure before that night, and I believe it was because of the ashes in the house.

The next day, I walked into every room in the house and prayed the "Lord's Prayer," asking God to eradicate the dark and unsettling entity from the home. I also told the dark entity that they were unwelcome there and needed to leave. After that day, I didn't see the dark entity come back. A couple of months later, however, when my roommate moved out and took the urn of ashes with him, there was an even deeper sense of peace in the house.

I experienced another instance where ashes of a living being brought forth a spirit visit. This one, however, was a good spirit – it was my puppy Buzz Wyatt. Buzz was tragically killed on February 22, 2005, at the age of 7 months, when his leash opened and he dashed out in front of an oncoming speeding car. I had Buzz's ashes put inside a small wooden box, with a gold name plate, which I keep in the house next to his pictures and a photo album dedicated to him.

Buzz has given me many signs including moving objects and making pennies appear, and I've actually even seen a full body apparition of him. The signs that Buzz has given me appear in Chapter 17 of this book.

CHAPTER 5
Getting Rid of Earth-bound Ghosts and Negative Energy

I admit that I'm not very experienced in ridding a home of Earth-bound ghosts or negative energy, but I've read the writings of others and have had a couple of successes. As I mentioned previously, when my ex-roommate's mother's dark spirit appeared in my home, I was able to get her to leave until the urn with her ashes was finally removed from the house.

I suggest doing what I did to remove the dark energy I encountered. I walked into each room in the house and prayed the Lord's Prayer out loud. I also asked the dark spirit to leave. It's important to tell the dark entity that they are not welcome there, and that you live in that space now. After I did all of this, the dark entity never reappeared, and when the urn was removed a deeper sense of peace came into the house.

My mother told me that when she was a little girl growing up in East Boston, Massachusetts, people would have a priest come into a house and bless it, to keep the evil spirits away and bring love and peace to the house.

Earth-bound ghosts can attach themselves to people, just like they can attach themselves to a home they lived in or a piece of furniture that they loved. They love negative energy and feed off it. So, if you're with someone who is negative much of the time and sickly often, they may in fact, have a dark entity or ghost attached to them.

Various experts have said that because we all have auras that are different colors, depending on the attitude and heart of the person, we need to picture our aura as very bright when trying to protect ourselves from or rid ourselves of bad entities. Picture in your mind that you are surrounded by God's white light and it will serve as a kind of "barrier" from the negative energy.

The same holds true when trying to get a ghost to pass into the light. Some mediums say that you need to picture a "white light" in part of the room where an Earth-bound ghost is, and instruct them to go into the light. Or, as I have done in several cases when I've run into ghosts, you can tell them to seek out a nearby funeral home. Yes, ghosts can sense funeral homes. Remember, ghosts "power up" based on energy, emotional or otherwise, and where do you find a lot of emotion? You find them at funeral homes, where people are severely grieving over the loss of a loved one. That's also where people's spirits go until after the wake, and it's there they pass into the light.

For further reading, I strongly recommend Mary Ann Winkowski's book *When Ghosts Speak*. She suggests using sea salt, smudge sticks, and plants like marigolds, Cyprus, myrrh, rosemary, geraniums, violets and more. A simple exercise recommends drying the geranium flowers, making sachets and putting them in the corners of the rooms of the dwelling where a ghost is lingering.

Winkowski has entire chapters in her book devoted to ridding a person, house or object of a ghost or negative energy, and I strongly recommend it. I also recommend not trying to do this yourself, unless you know how to protect yourself from negative spirits. It would be wise to either contact a medium or a religious figure to bless the house and cleanse it.

CHAPTER 6
How Can People Experience Ghosts?

People who don't believe in ghosts or strange, unexplainable happenings haven't experienced them or refuse to acknowledge them. Although I've mentioned that I believe the ability to be a medium is genetic, I think everyone can tap into the energy and develop a level of ability. One way to do so is to be open-minded and optimistic, and not try to find "logical" explanations for everything. Sometimes there just aren't logical explanations for things.

There are different ways to experience messages from ghosts and spirits. For example, you can see them in full form, as a shadow, or ectoplasm. You can also feel them as cold sensations or electrical impulses (i.e. causing the hair on your arms to stand up).You may also be able to hear them either as audible or in your head. How can you tell if you're hearing a ghost talk to you y thoughts? If you have thoughts that don't seem to be your own, they may be from a spirit or ghost trying to communicate. Thoughts are energy, and ghosts and spirits are beings of energy, so it makes sense that we're able communicate in that way from the living to the dead and vice versa.

For example, I was walking our dogs one day, and a spirit named "Dave" came to me as I passed by a certain house. The spirit only kept repeating his name in my head as I continued walking and didn't share any more information. I pondered if I was sub-consciously trying to remember if I was supposed to call anyone named Dave. However, I don't work with anyone named Dave and haven't spoken to anyone with that name for a long time. It was, in fact, a spirit trying to communicate.

Another way spirits communicate is what we may deem as a coincidence. There are no such things as coincidences. If you're walking down the street and bump into someone, start talking and find something in common, that's not a coincidence. More likely, it was planned by a spirit that's watching over you. If a friend calls you when you're thinking of them, or a song you were just thinking of comes on the radio, that's not a coincidence. Someone in the spirit world is sending you a message. Some people report their phone ringing and no one on the other end, and nothing showing up on caller I.D., when even blocked numbers come up "private." Spirits have been known to call loved ones from the other side.

Every person we meet in this lifetime adds something to our experience on Earth, be it good or bad. I had a relationship with a person who was mentally abusive and totally selfish, but I took lessons from that and grew from it. Negative things that happen to us are meant to happen, so we can learn from them. All people on Earth are in various stages of learning about life and love. You may not immediately know the reason why you've gone somewhere you may not have wanted to go, done something you may not have wanted to do, or met someone that you wonder why you did, but you will likely find out the reasons later.

An example of this is when Tom and I were invited to a Christmas party in 2006. We were both exhausted and it was a Friday night, so we hesitated about going, but at the last minute decided we couldn't miss it. It was at the time in my life when I was trying to get a better handle on my abilities to detect or understand the spirit world. We went, and it was there that we met a young woman named Sarah whom I was apparently supposed to meet. At the party, she told me that she has a unique ability to foresee deaths. She said that she had dreamed of a couple of people who wound up passing to the other side, a short time after she dreamt of them. I thought that was an interesting and scary ability. What it told me was that we all have certain "gifts" and truly can speak with those beyond to get and understand messages.

It doesn't take talent or being special to experience "supernatural" things. What it does take, however, is being unafraid to be emotional in your life, to love, to live and enjoy the blessings around you and form close bonds with others. It has been said that people who experience emotions on a deep level tend to be the ones who see spirits or experience things that most others do not. In addition, people who have positive attitudes and are optimistic and loving tend to tune in to spirits more easily than those who do or are not.

I've found that in general, cynical and negative people cannot experience ghosts. Those people, however, are not closed to experiences. Spirits who have passed to the other side can communicate with anyone in their dreams. When we're dreaming, the rational, logical thinking mind is at rest, and we are more "open-minded." It's then that a spirit that has already passed can finally make contact with us.

Many people do experience signs from their loved ones who have passed on. I often tell people who lose a loved one that they need to look for signs. It doesn't matter if the one that passed was a human or animal. They're still a spirit and can still communicate.

People who have passed will leave pennies or change around us. Someone told me that, and when my puppy Buzz passed away, I found change every day for almost a year. When my partner Tom's grandmother passed away, suddenly he started finding pennies, nickels, dimes and quarters. He jokes that his grandmother should know about inflation and start leaving dollar bills. Every now and then, she still sends Tom monetary reminders that she's still around.

PEOPLE WHO EXPERIENCE GHOSTS AND SPIRITS, AND HOW

There are two kinds of people who experience ghosts and spirits. The first type of person sees only Earth-bound spirits. One famous such person is Mary Ann Winkowski, who is an author and consultant on the television show "Ghost Whisperer." Mary Ann wrote in her book *When Ghosts Speak* that she's been able to see and talk with ghosts since she was a little girl.

A second kind of person is a medium like James Van Praagh or Lisa Williams. Van Praagh wrote in his book *Ghosts Among Us* that he mostly communicates with spirits that have crossed over into the light. He typically doesn't interact with Earth-bound spirits, although he did mention some encounters. I believe that everyone is a medium in terms of being able to communicate with loved ones from their own family or who they were very close to making them what I think of as "limited mediums."

Like Van Praagh and Williams, I seem to be able to do both. I can sense Earth-bound ghosts for the most part, but also have been able to sense/feel the spirits that have crossed over.

What all mediums have in common is that they have a strong faith and heightened emotions and are open-minded. Optimistic, happy people are a lot more likely to communicate with spirits than negative people.

It's also interesting to note that people who are optimistic and positive have better control when spirits are present. People who are negative add to a ghost's energy. Ghosts feed off of negative energy such as fear, anger and anxiety.

WAYS IN WHICH SPIRITS AND GHOSTS ARE "RECEIVED"

There are quite a number of ways that people can sense or communicate with spirits. They can be clairsentient, clairvoyant, clairaudient, or receive what is called inspirational thought.

People or mediums who can read spirits can be more than one of the above. I believe that although my abilities are limited and not yet fully developed, I've experienced clairsentience, clairvoyance and clairaudience.

Clairsentience means that you can basically sense when a spirit is in the room. It's happened to me many times, such as in historic homes that I've toured. It also means that you can feel the spirit's personality and emotions, as I did on several occasions when the mothers of three different friends came through to me. Sometimes you can also feel the way that a ghost or spirit died. I've experienced several ghosts' deaths, including heart attack and shortness of breath. When that happens, it's important to tell the ghost you understand how they passed and that they need to stop sharing their symptoms.

Merriam-Webster's online dictionary defines *Clairvoyance* as "the power or faculty of discerning objects not present to the senses" or the "ability to perceive matters beyond the range of ordinary perception." People who have this ability see spirits, people, colors, objects and even scenes that a spirit wants them to see in order to communicate thoughts or ideas to the medium. It's not actually seeing these things in a room, for example, but rather seeing in your mind.

Clairaudience means to hear clearly. Van Praagh mentioned that it's like hearing something at a higher vibration, such as a dog hears things that a human cannot. The sounds are like music, speaking, laughter and more. If you own a dog, and you find him staring at a wall, for example, he may have tuned into a spirit. I've watched my dog Dolly stare at part of an empty room, and sensed that my late dog Buzz was in the room.

In October of 2008, my partner and I went to see medium and clairvoyant Lisa Williams at the Lyric Opera house in Baltimore, Maryland. Lisa has achieved fame on television and touring with her abilities. She had a program on Lifetime television in 2007 and 2008 and maintains a blog and a web site at *www.lisawilliamsmedium.com.*

That night as we watched and listened intently, Lisa heard spirits talking with her from both sides of the stage. She said that in the case of several spirits talking at the same time, the strongest personality would come through. During the show, she would lean toward one side of the stage or the other, depending on where the strongest spirit was.

She also mentioned that sometimes different spirits speak to her at the same time, making it hard to discern if something being said was from the same ghost or spirit. Several times throughout the show, she asked the person in the audience that she was reading about a detail she just "heard." If the person couldn't relate, it became apparent that another spirit was speaking to her, trying to reach someone else in the audience. Being clairaudient isn't like hearing an actual sound. It's more like someone is speaking in your head and you "hear it" with your mind: thus, it's sometimes hard to discern if it comes from one person or another.

The one thing that helps separate multiple spirits who are communicating at the same time is their personalities. The personality that a person had during their life on Earth is still with them when they pass. So once a spirit continues speaking, the clairaudient person "hearing them" can realize when something being said is coming from one spirit in particular, based on their personality traits.

The fourth kind of communication concerns how spirits can influence people to do things, such as writing or art. This is called *Inspirational Thought*. A spirit will convey to a medium knowledge or impressions. What's interesting about this communication is that the emotion involved with a "clairaudient" experience isn't there. It strikes me as more like straight reading out of a book. It's been noted that "inspirational thought" from spirits may have been given to great painters, inventors or composers.

So what kind of people can't see spirits? Closed-minded, logical, non-believers will never see a spirit or have an experience, other than in their dreams. When a person is asleep, their mind is opened and their logical reasoning side is asleep. That's when those people can and have reported dreaming of their loved ones appearing in their dreams. It's the only time a spirit who has passed can communicate with someone who "doesn't believe" in spirits.

Closed-minded people, however, may experience Earth-bound ghosts. If they go into a place they know to be haunted and have a small fear of what may be lurking in the place, they create negative energy. That negative energy is all that's needed to help an Earth-bound ghost manifest itself.

If you've ever watched the short-lived television program called "Scariest Places on Earth," which was broadcast on the Sci-Fi Channel (now the SyFy Channel) in early 2008, there were a lot of non-believers that had experiences. That's because some in the group had fear and anxiety and powered up the Earth-bound ghosts that resided in those places.

Another television program that has remained popular and that I enjoy is "Ghost Hunters," also on the SyFy Channel. In this program people use scientific equipment, such as infrared cameras, to detect heat and cold signatures and electronic recorders to capture "electronic voice phenomenon (EVP)" in order to scientifically prove there may be an entity in a place. Becoming a "Ghost Hunter" is another way that people who are too logical in their thinking, or unable to open their minds can encounter the paranormal.

ECTOPLASM

Ghosts are well known for materializing as "ectoplasm." According to Wikipedia, "Ectoplasm (from the Greek ektos, "outside," and plasma, "something formed or molded") is a term coined by Charles Richet to denote a substance or spiritual energy "exteriorized" by physical mediums. Ectoplasm has been associated with the formation of ghosts and hypothesized to be an enabling factor in "psychokinesis."

Ectoplasm is the image that people generally have of ghosts. That's usually what photographs pick up: white, gray or transparent images. Some physical mediums have been seen "oozing" ectoplasm when connecting to a spirit. Ectoplasm looks like a mist.

ELECTRONIC VOICE PHENOMENA (EVP)

The idea of electronic voice phenomena or EVP was popularized by parapsychologist Konstantin Raudive. Wikipedia says that electronic voice phenomena are "sections of static noise on the radio or electronic recording media that are interpreted by paranormal investigators as voices speaking words usually attributed to ghosts or spirits."

Professional Ghost Hunters now use digital recording devices to pick up sounds at higher frequencies that cannot be heard by the human ear. It's possible that dogs may even hear spirits when they speak, although humans may not, simply because dogs hear at higher frequencies than humans. According to Stanley Coren in *How Dogs Think*, humans hear up to about 12,000 Hertz, while the highest ranges some dogs can hear ranges as high as 47,000 to 60,000 Hertz. Hertz is the equivalent of cycles of sound waves per second.

EVPs are generally brief. They are usually only a word or a couple of words. On the popular "Ghost Hunters" show, the crew would frequently pick up EVPs. In one instance, they recorded a deep male voice actually telling them to get out of the prison they were working in. Some paranormal investigators have said that EVPs may be leftover psychic energies from a past event.

Many organizations study EVPs and publish articles and research. Some organizations include: The American Association of Electronic Voice Phenomena, the International Ghost Hunters Society, The Rorschach Audio Project, Interdisciplinary Laboratory for Biopsychocybernetics Research and the Journal of the Society for Psychical Research, based in the United Kingdom. All of these can be found through Internet searches.

CHAPTER 7
How I Experience Ghosts and Spirits

How do I experience ghosts? I've experienced both Earth-bound ghosts and spirits (who have passed into the light and come back with messages) with a number of senses. I've seen only a couple of full-body apparitions, the first one being my grandfather six months after he died in 1976.

I've also hear ghosts and spirits, either as sounds they create or when they speak to me in my mind.

When I was in my 30s in the 1990s, I became interested in reading stories about ghosts. Before that, I was too unsettled and unfocused. I couldn't "tune in" to what was happening around me because I was trying to get my life together. In fact, when I was 34 years old, I went back to school in Kentucky for a third degree, and then I started experiencing ghosts. Why? I believe that my head and my heart were finally settled on a direction in life, which was pursuing a career related to meteorology (in which I still work today).

It was in Kentucky that I had a couple of ghostly experiences that I'll never forget. I mention those in the next chapter. After those experiences, I started reading books about Earth-bound ghosts. I was trying to understand why they appear, who they may be, what they're doing on Earth and why they didn't pass into the light. But reading ghost stories only gave me some of the answers of why ghosts remain Earth-bound.

In 1996-1997 when I was feeling more settled in my mind and heart, I started sensing ghosts again. My experiences included seeing, hearing, sensing and feeling them. The feelings ranged from experiencing actual cold spots to a physical feeling, such as when the spirit of my friend's grandmother made a corner of the bed go down that I was lying in. I explain that story in Chapter 9: Messages via Water.

Since 2006, when I fell in love, my emotions and senses have been heightened and continue to increase. I've since been able to sense spirits around much more often. Although I haven't always been able to tell what sex or age they are, I could tell we weren't alone.

In March 2008, I wrote to psychic medium Mary Ann Winkowski about trying to refine my abilities to help ghosts cross over. In a personal letter back to me, she wrote about my relationship with Tom: "How very wonderful that you are in such a marvelous relationship. This surely has helped you to enhance your abilities. I wish you many-

many happy years together." I have learned that falling in love heightens your emotional levels and makes you act as kind of a "tuning fork" for receiving spiritual energies and signals.

This makes sense because when you're in love, you radiate a positive emotional energy, and spirits pick up on emotional energy, whether positive or negative. However, ghosts can use the negative energy and get stronger. Positive energy tends to act as a shield or a barrier to keep ghosts at a distance.

For the most part, though, my experiences have been very strong feelings. How I've come to know that there's a ghost or a spirit around me is that I develop a headache in the lower left side of the back of my head.

What's interesting about my headache "signal" is that medium Mary Ann Winkowski said in her book *When Ghosts Speak* that one of her two daughters, Tara, also has her ability, and she, like me, develops headaches whenever ghosts are around. I have a theory that the headaches may be caused by the "electricity" or charge that ghosts have. When you're around a high electromagnetic field given off by an electric outlet in your home, it can produce headaches, dizziness, etc.

In episodes of "Ghost Hunters" on the SyFy Channel, the TAPS group uses EMF meters, electro-magnetic field detectors to help determine if there's a ghost in a room, or if there's an electric appliance that's giving off high readings.

Usually after my dull headache starts, I begin to get a picture in my mind of the person communicating to me. Then they tell me things. There have been children and adults, men and women, and the information has been pretty accurate. Tom is always trying to disprove me, but he and I usually wind up verifying the type of person or persons who are coming through to me, by checking news or historical records.

I've mentioned Mary Ann Winkowski a number of times. That's because she brought an awakening to me of my abilities. I had the good fortune to meet Mary Ann in person in Lutherville, Maryland at a book signing at Borders Books on April 11, 2008. I also corresponded with her afterward, and she gave me some good advice when I asked her about refining my abilities.

She told me in her letter, "First, you have to be comfortable with your ability. What I mean by this is that you have to believe in what you do and have confidence in yourself. This is sometimes difficult. There are many people who will try to make you feel uncomfortable with what you do. Always believe in yourself and what you can do."

She's absolutely right. I've met a lot of skeptics in my life, but when I've been able to provide proof of the ghost or spirit's existence, either by identifying their age, sex, or something else, then skeptics have an awakening of sorts.

Further, Mary Ann told me, "I would recommend reading and studying as much as possible. I was drawn to the works of Edgar Cayce and Ruth Montgomery. I always recommend these writers, but please do not limit myself to my choices. There is a cornucopia of written works available."

Refining your ability takes patience and faith. You must also allow yourself to be open-minded. As I mentioned in the last chapter, closed-minded people do not "allow" themselves to be open to spirit communications other than through dreams.

As Ms. Winkowski said in her letter to me, "I wish I had the magic formula that I could use to help people grow their gifts to their full potential, but I do not. It takes work, patience, and a lot of faith."

CHAPTER 8
My Life Among Ghosts and Spirits

AN INHERITED ABILITY

The ability to see or sense spirits apparently goes back a couple of generations in my family. My great-grandparents apparently had it, my mother has it, and I do as well. In her book *We Are Their Heaven*, medium Allison DuBois said that her three little girls all have her ability, and that she also believes being a medium is genetic." Medium Concetta Bertoldi of New Jersey has also said that the "gift" runs in the family, and it was present on her father's side. In Chapter 18: Ghost / Spirit Stories From Others, you'll read about another mother and son whom both have sensed spirits.

When my grandmother Sarina was alive, she told my mother, her sister and brother an interesting story about her home town. Sarina was born in Avelino, a small town near Naples, Italy, in the Campania region in 1899. She grew up there until the early 1900s when she came to America. She said that her parents would tell her that everyone in the town knew each other, because it was a very small town. She went on to say that the townspeople knew when someone died, and would actually see the ghosts of people who had already passed away still walking around the streets and among the living.

My mother told me of her first encounter with a spirit, after her mother, Sarina passed away. She married my grandfather, another Italian, who grew up in Boston, Massachusetts. Sarina gave birth to two girls and a boy. My mother was, of course, one of those girls, and she was born with some amazing abilities.

My mother is psychic and had an auditory visit from my grandmother once my grandmother passed into the light. Mom tells the story this way: "It was almost a year after my mother passed away, when she came to me. I was lying in bed and Ed (my dad) was in the bathroom shaving." She said that she was very relaxed and sleepy, laying on her left side. She heard very loudly, and clearly, her mother Sarina saying (in broken English, because she spoke mostly Italian when she was alive) her name "Norma" in her right ear. My mother said "I was so scared that I got up immediately and ran down the hall to the bathroom and ripped the tee-shirt off your father's back." She said that after she calmed down, she realized her mother was trying to tell her that she's in a good place, and that she was fine. No matter how many times my mother asked her mother Sarina to come back and talk to her, she never returned. Apparently, Sarina didn't want to again scare her daughter.

Since I was a small child, mom has always known things that she couldn't have possibly known beforehand. She always believed she was psychic, and I believe it, too.

In 2008, I finally learned from my mother of two supernatural experiences that my mother's father, my grandfather Giramondo, had when he was alive. One involved actually feeling a spirit, the other involved orbs.

My mother told me that in the 1930s and 1940s, when she lived with her brother and sister and parents in East Boston, Massachusetts, the house had a coal furnace in the basement to provide heat to the house. One evening, Giramondo went down into the dark basement to shovel more coal into the furnace in the dark basement. As he was feeling his way to the furnace along the wall, he touched the sleeve of a woman's garment, on the body of a person standing there! She said Giramondo asked if it was his deceased aunt Elvina, and she replied, "yes." My mother didn't tell me if my grandfather wound up shoveling the coal into the furnace or ran back upstairs.

Another story involving my grandfather occurred after his wife Sarina passed in 1958. Sarina was buried in a cemetery in West Roxbury, Massachusetts. Later that year or the next year when my grandfather Giramondo went to visit, he saw what he told my mother was a "ring of fire" over the gravesite. Most likely, it was an orb (spirit). This orb or orbs was likely triggered by my grandfather's arrival, as his emotional energy could have enabled the spirit to become visible. When the energy is removed, the orb likely disappeared.

My mother also told me an interesting story as I was writing this book in 2008. When my grandfather Giramondo, died in the harsh New England winter of 1976, he couldn't be buried because the ground was frozen. He was supposed to be buried in a plot next to my grandmother Sarina when the spring came and the ground thawed. However, my mother and father, who visited that cemetery every couple of months, and always have, said that they never remember the ground being dug up or disturbed after my grandfather passed.

Back in the late 1970s or early 1980s my mother's sister Tillie spoke with my mother about the "untouched" grave and went to a psychic to get answers. The psychic told Tillie that Giramondo was never buried. Further, the psychic said that he was cremated, but couldn't tell where his ashes were.

As it turns out, there were stories of some funeral homes in New England that were cremating people who should've been buried, and in one case in New Hampshire, the funeral home was mixing up the ashes. My mother thinks the psychic could be correct that my grandfather is still trying to find that peace, as she said she's seen the figure of a man around her house (that she and my dad have lived in since 1962), dressed in black. She believes that man to be my grandfather. Although they haven't yet had the gravesite dug up to confirm the psychic's feelings, it's easy to believe that my grandfather has been trying to tell my mother something for years and is still trying. That leads me to my first experience with the supernatural.

Late in 2009 when I was editing this book, my mother found an old newspaper clipping from 1980 containing an obituary of one of my mother's cousins. My mother read the obituary to me over the phone, and added more proof that my mediumistic abilities have come from my family.

My mother's father had several siblings and one of them was a sister, Edith. Edith had a daughter also named Edith. It was her obituary that my mother found. The obituary from the *Patriot Ledger newspaper* of Quincy, Massachusetts read as follows: "Edith E. (Scimone) Locke [she had married twice], 59, of Florida, formerly of Randolph, an astrologer, died Saturday at Milton hospital." The obituary went on to say "In an article in the Patriot Ledger in 1980, Mrs. Locke told how she used her experience as an astrologer who helped police solve crimes."

This was quite a surprise to me that my mother's cousin was a psychic medium who communicated with spirits and ghosts to solve crimes and help the local police.

So, in my family, my grandfather, my mother, my mother's cousin, and I have the ability to communicate with ghosts and spirits. It's just more proof that sometimes the ability to communicate with those who have passed may be genetic.

MY FIRST EXPERIENCE

My mother's father, Giramondo, died of pneumonia at the age of 76. The doctors told my mother that if he had come to the hospital a day before, they likely could have saved him.

My grandfather was an electrician and worked at shipyards in Massachusetts from the time my mother was born in the late 1920s until he retired. He was a learned man, who had a fascination with the unknown. I remember as a boy going over his house and seeing his bookcases with books about UFOs and other unexplained phenomena, although I can't recall if he had books on ghosts. I wouldn't be surprised if he did have some books on ghosts and spirits.

I don't remember visiting my grandfather and step-grandmother (my mother's mother passed before I was born and my granddad remarried) often as a boy. I do remember that the house always smelled of garlic, but that's because my grandfather was a true Italian and he must've put it in everything he cooked. I don't remember being particularly close to my grandfather, but my younger brother and I did sit with him and listen to him talk about UFOs and strange things. He had a very soft voice, too.

I remember the day of my grandfather's wake. It was held at a funeral home in Weymouth, Massachusetts, during a snow storm (typical in New England in winter). It was the first wake I ever attended, now that I think about it. I was 13 years old.

I don't remember what my grandfather looked like as he lay in "state," which I think is a good thing, because people never seem to look as they did when they were alive. We didn't go to the gravesite because the ground was frozen. I remember someone saying that he would be buried in the springtime when the ground thawed, and thought "I wonder where they're going to keep him." I tried not to think about that much afterward.

Months passed and spring and summer came. It was that summer my grandfather came to me, and I had my first experience with a ghost or spirit. I can't be sure if he passed or not because I was scared out of my wits and was too young to know any better.

It was a weekend day, early evening. My parents had gone out to run errands, and my brothers were out with their friends. I enjoyed staying home with our dog "Gigi," a poodle, of course (with a name like that you think it would be a bulldog?). I used to create ideas for superheroes and write and draw my own comic books. I would sit for hours doing it.

I remember that it started getting dark outside, and it must have been twilight. I was sitting in our kitchen at the table in a direction that faced the length of the house. I could see directly into the dining room and farther into the living room. We had a fireplace at the far wall on the living room. I remember looking up into the very dark living room, and glancing at the fireplace which was in the center of the wall. That's when I saw little "globes" of white light start streaming from the sides of the room and clustering together in the center of the room, directly in front of the fireplace. I was in total disbelief about what I was seeing but I still sat there, our poodle at my side, sitting on the kitchen bench with me.

It had to be within a minute, but it seemed much longer than that, when the "clusters" of white light took shape in the room's center. It then took on color and form, and before me was standing my grandfather! I have chills as I write this. I was totally shocked and surprised. I was also really scared, so I grabbed my drawings and the dog and ran outside. I was afraid to go back inside so I sat on the steps outside my parents' house until they pulled up the driveway about an hour later. They asked what I was doing outside with the dog, and I told them what happened. I don't know if they believed me or not, but I know what I saw. I was really scared.

If I knew then what I know now, I would have walked up to him and tried to communicate. Perhaps, my grandfather was trying to confirm what the psychic told my aunt, about my grandfather not being buried in his plot. I don't know. What I do know is that my grandfather has not come back to me since. Why? Because he scared me and is likely afraid to do it again, even though I'm now at a different level of understanding.

CHAPTER 9
Messages Vla Water

VOICE IN THE SHOWER

In December 2007, my friend Kathy in central Florida told me of the sudden passing of her mother Pat after kidney failure brought on by an arthritis medication. According to Kathy, her mother had been in decent health before taking the medication. Her death was devastating to Kathy, who had lived with her mom for over three decades. Her mom was her best friend.

After learning of Pat's passing, I called Kathy from Maryland and told her that her mother's spirit would let her know that she has safely passed on and that she should look for signs. Six months later, her mother Pat, whom I had never met, gave me a big sign, hundreds of miles away from Kathy.

I worked with Kathy in a hotel in central Florida in 1995 and stayed in touch with her ever since. In fact, I write a quarterly personal newsletter, print it, and mail it to my friends around the U.S. I would always write little notes on it and direct some comments to Pat, because she and Kathy would both read it. Kathy told me that her mom always enjoyed reading about my latest adventures, so that's how she knew me. Of course, in a couple of newsletters, I'd briefly mention my ghostly/spiritual encounters. That must've stayed with her because she came to me to give Kathy a message.

Friday, June 20, 2008, was an ordinary work day. It was, however, an extraordinary night. After dinner and walking our dogs, I took a shower to get ready for bed. Water enables spirits to communicate, and this was proof. As I was showering, Kathy's mother Pat came into my mind, and I heard her say "Call Kathy now!" She said it twice. I said aloud in the shower "Okay, I'll call her!" My partner, in the other room thought I was crazy talking to myself in the shower.

I got out of the shower and toweled dry, and said aloud, "It's late, maybe I'll call her tomorrow." Immediately, Pat came back to me and said in my head, "No, you'll call her tonight." So, I dialed Kathy's number. I hadn't spoken or emailed Kathy in about a month, so I had no idea what was happening with her.

Kathy said that in the 6 months since her mother's death, that very day had been one of the most emotionally difficult for her for some reason. She said she broke down and was an emotional wreck. Obviously, her mom knew this and needed me to pass some messages.

My conversation with Kathy was mostly my telling Kathy what her mom was telling me. "Kathy, you need to get out this weekend and be around people," I was telling her, as her mother was telling me. "You need to stop grieving and start living." I stopped for a minute and said, "Kathy, your mother is very feisty. She even came to me in the shower." Further, I said, "Your mother is telling you to "shit or get off the pot and get your life together!" I didn't believe I was saying this, but Kathy said, "That sounds like my mother!"

When I asked Kathy why she thinks her mother came to me, she said that her family has been distant since her mother's death. Kathy reasoned that her mom knew that I would be the one to call her with her mom's message. I was.

Three days later, I heard back from Kathy, and she had taken her mom's advice. She sounded a whole lot better. The bottom line is that sometimes we need to be reminded that our loved ones are in a better place, and we need to stop dwelling on the loss. We need to cherish the good memories and get on with our lives, knowing they're around us, love us and will protect us.

DRAWING WATER ENERGY TO SIT ON A BED

Another incident occurred in 2000, when I was living in Marietta, Georgia. My friend Jeff who had lost his grandmother a couple of years before moved into an apartment with me.

PHOTO: Jeff's Grandma Bonney.
Credit: Jeff F.

Jeff and his grandmother were very close and shared a special bond. Jeff had a very difficult time accepting her death even years later.

I think it was within the first month after Jeff had moved in that I was lying in my bed, trying to get to sleep. The door from the bedroom was opened into the hallway, and Jeff had just gone into the shower in the bathroom, which was adjacent to the bedroom.

While he was showering, I remember lying on the bed and

closing my eyes. That's when I actually felt the far left corner of the bed go down as if someone were sitting on it. I remember that my eyes were still closed, so I thought it was Jeff and called out his name. Because there was no response, I opened my eyes and there was no one there. In fact, the corner of the bed started coming back up! That's when I heard the water still running in the bathroom shower and realized Jeff was still taking a shower.

I looked around and felt a very calming presence standing next to me on the right side of the bed (the side I was on). I realized it was Jeff's grandmother. In my mind's eye, she told me to tell Jeff, "It will be all right," and that she's always around to watch over Jeff. She must've used the energy in the water to come through, but at that time, I had no idea that water was a medium in which spirits could manifest themselves.

As with Kathy's mother, I had also never met Jeff's grandmother. I didn't even know Jeff at the time of his grandmother's passing.

When Jeff finished showering and came out of the bathroom, I called him over and told him what happened. He immediately broke down. I think that he needed to hear that his Nana was okay and that she was indeed looking out for him.

CHAPTER 10
My Dad and Many Lessons He Taught Me About the Afterlife

On August 2, 2008, during the time I was writing this book, my dad suddenly and shockingly passed away from a stroke. It was a devastating experience I will never forget, as any child can tell you when they lose a parent.

As that horrible week progressed my dad told me he was okay and wanted me to share that with my mother. There were other amazing things that happened that truly showed that a spirit was helping protect and guide my mother during the time of my dad's stroke.

My partner and I live about 400 miles away from my younger brother and we received a phone call from him around 8 p.m. EDT on Saturday, August 2, as he was driving to the hospital in central Massachusetts where my dad was taken by ambulance.

My brother informed me that my parents were out shopping after enjoying a dinner about 45 minutes west of their home. Here's an instance of two things that are just too amazing to be a coincidence. There was definitely a spiritual guide that was looking out for my mother during this tragic event.

SPIRITS WATCHING OVER MY MOTHER

My parents had gone out to eat dinner, as they usually did on Saturday nights. On that day, they decided to go to a restaurant that was about 45 minutes away, which also happens to be close to where my older brother lives.

After dinner, they decided to go shopping at Kohl's department store in Framingham, Massachusetts. After shopping, they came back to the car, and dad searched his pockets for his keys. Instead, he found a hole in his pocket, and assumed his keys slipped out in the store. Interestingly enough, the keys didn't slip out while they were at the restaurant or before they went into the store.

So, my mom waited at the car while dad ambled back toward the front door of the store to ask if someone turned in his keys. My mother grew concerned when dad didn't come back after a short time, so she started walking back toward the store. She looked down and saw my dad lying in the grass, grasping the grass with his hand. He had had a stroke and couldn't speak. My mother screamed for help.

A woman in the parking lot (with a cell phone) ran over to my mother. After calling 911, she asked mom for a phone number of a nearby relative. My mother couldn't remember my older brother's phone number. When the woman asked my brother's name, coincidentally, the woman knew who he was through a friend of hers.

The woman called her friend and got my older brother's phone number. She then called him and told him what had happened, and he raced over to the store to meet up with my mother and the ambulance.

That was NO coincidence that this woman, who lives two towns away from my older brother, had a friend who knew him. That was divine intervention. A spirit who was watching out for my mother provided this incredible link.

My dad had passed either in the ambulance or by the time he arrived at the hospital.

WHO WAS MY DAD?

My dad was born November 8, 1928. He was the only child in his family, although he had a brother who died at birth before my dad was born. Dad grew up in Massachusetts and did a stint as a U.S. Military Policeman in the Army during the Korean War. He also played the trumpet in the army and in nightclubs. He led a big band called "Buddies." Buddy was his nickname. He and mom married on June 19, 1955. They had three boys, and I am the middle son.

Dad worked in the insurance industry, graduated from Boston University and was an avid Red Sox fan.

Dad loved candy. His car was loaded with it. After he passed away, my family even found some candy in his closet. He loved those orange circus peanuts, Jujubes, gummy bears. He was also famous for making popcorn and eating peanuts or ice cream late before bed.

My dad was the most patient man I've ever known. I learned a lot from my dad: patience, tolerance, love.

Dad loved reading mysteries and espionage books. That's where I got my love for reading. When my younger brother and I were kids, Dad would take us with him every Saturday to do errands and stop at a local drugstore to buy us superhero comic books. Mom hated for us to keep bringing them home, so Dad had us roll them up in our sleeves and walk in the house. We'd promptly disappear into the bedroom and would read them together.

My Dad loved to write. Since I left Massachusetts in 1989 to live in other states Dad wrote letters to me a couple of times a month and I've kept every letter. Those are priceless to me. Dad inspired me to write, and now I make a living doing it.

Dad was extremely well known throughout New England in the insurance industry. He worked in it for about 50 years and even taught classes. Despite his being "retired" he still loved working part time. In fact, during Dad's last week on Earth an insurance company called and asked him to work for them part time. He worked 4 out of the 5 days. That was my Dad - he had a great work ethic.

My dad also had a subtle sense of humor. I remember two most recent incidents from my visits before he passed. The first occurred at Christmas 2007, when Tom and I and the dogs were up visiting. My Mom said to my Dad that he forgot to do something, and he raised his hand, waved it backward at my mother, and said "Baaaaah" as he walked away. That was really funny, and now Tom and I do it to each other.

In the fall of 2007 when Tom and I were visiting my parents, we all went to Home Depot together. We were walking around the garden shop with them and looking at all the plants. At one point, Tom and I were all the way down the aisle from where my parents were looking at plants. Suddenly, my Mom bumped into a plant and knocked it over. We immediately heard Dad say loudly, "Norma did it!" and we laughed out loud.

In addition to all of these characteristics, Dad loved his grandchildren, grand-dogs, and his wife and kids. At the wake, some of his co-workers told us, "he lived for (his wife) Norma. He would always talk about doing whatever made Norma happy, because it made him happy."

DAD'S COMMUNICATIONS DURING THE WEEK

Tom and I and our dogs drove from Maryland to Massachusetts and arrived at my mother's house on Monday, August 4, on the second day after Dad's passing. We spent the next two days helping make arrangements with my brothers for the funeral home and church.

On Tuesday, my mom asked why she couldn't dream of my dad. I explained to her that he hadn't passed into the light yet and would do so after the funeral. Once he's in the light, he'll be able to come to her in her dreams. Earth-bound ghosts are not able to communicate through dreams, only those who have passed into the light can do that.

Wednesday, August 6, was the day of the wake. The funeral director was incredible. She thought of everything and even sent a full course dinner for 10 over to my mother's house the night before. My family, consisting of my mother, my two brothers and their wives, and my partner and I, arrived at the funeral home at 3 p.m. It was unnerving walking in that front left room of the Lydon Funeral Home. The open casket was at the far end of the room, and I could see my dad's body in it. As anyone can attest, it's a shock to see your loved one in that state. I kept trying to focus on the fact that he's okay, and his spirit is most likely around. I know that everyone sticks around for their wake and funeral, and my dad let me know that this was to be no different from what I've heard.

Just before the visiting hours for Dad's wake began, I had our entire family sign a note in the last paperback novel he was in the middle of reading, Brad Thor's book *The First Commandment*, and we put it inside the casket with him. Also, because he loved the Red Sox (baseball), my younger brother and his wife had their young sons sign "I love you, Papa" on a baseball, which they also put in the casket.

The wake began at 4 p.m. and people began filing in.

My younger brother is in local politics, so police and sheriff and local politicians came, in addition to friends, co-workers, and extended family.

As usual when I'm in the presence of a spirit or Earth-bound ghost, I developed a headache in the lower back left part of my head. I sensed my dad. He was standing at the foot of his casket looking at himself as people started filing in and past it. He watched them greet the receiving line of family members with my mom at the front. I sensed after awhile that Dad went over and stood next to my mother while she was greeting people; then he sat in a chair across from where Tom and I were standing while the Knights of Columbus and then the Morrisette Post legionnaires did prayer tributes to him. He seemed pleased and honored by those. He let me know that he was there and that he was okay. He was concerned about my mother's well-being, as he had been so devoted to her in life.

The wake ended at 8 p.m. and everyone dispersed. I'm not sure where my dad went at that time.

The next day was the funeral. I was dreading that because of how emotional it was going to be for everyone. We all met at the funeral home at 10 a.m. to say our last goodbyes. Before we left for the funeral at a Catholic Church about 5 minutes down the street, I struggled to read my tribute to my dad (that I had written on my blog the night he died). I opted to do mine at the funeral home, because it was both funny and serious, and I knew the setting would be better for it there. I ended my tribute by reading the last letter Dad wrote me dated June 18, 2008. We then left for the funeral.

My mom, Tom and I were seated in the front pew of the church, with mom in between the two of us. My brothers and their wives were behind us in the second pew, because each of them gave their eulogies at church.

My dad really came through during his funeral mass. My mom was crying hard at one point and holding tissues over her face. My dad came into my head and said "Tell your mother to use my handkerchief." My dad always carried handkerchiefs; mom never did. She didn't like them and thought they were gross. I leaned over and whispered to her what my Dad had just told me. My mother looked at me with a look of surprise and shock and said "How did you know I have a handkerchief in my pocket?" Answer: I didn't know. My dad told me. I told my mom that Dad was there and he told me to tell her that. She pulled out the hanky and used it, and it calmed her to know he was there. I was as surprised as my mother was, because I knew that in 45 years I'd never seen her use a handkerchief.

My mom knows and understands that I'm a medium. If she didn't believe me before, she certainly believed me then. I also sensed that my dad was standing behind my mom during a large part of the funeral mass, despite the fact that one of my sister-in-laws was physically sitting directly behind Mom. Spirits don't need physical space like we think of it.

Another sign I received from my dad was a feeling of how he died. I was still sitting in the pew next to my mom and Tom, and at one point, I felt a warm sensation in the left side of my chest become hot and spread through the left side of my chest and down my right arm. My dad passed from a stroke, and I have no idea what a stroke feels like and am unsure if this is how it may feel. I do know, however, that my dad was telling me that it was a heart issue that took him from Earth.

After the funeral, which was extremely difficult, as you would expect, we got back in the limousine and were driven to the cemetery, about 15 minutes away. I sensed that dad was driving with his body in the hearse ahead of us, and then he came back and sat with us in the limo. Although there were no physical seats left open, he was in there with us. As I mentioned, spirits don't need physical seats to be there.

At the gravesite, I was seated next to my mother and three other family members facing the casket, which was surrounded by flowers from the funeral home. All of this was under a tent on this cloudy, unusually cool August day in New England.

While the priest was reading at the casket and during the playing of Taps in the background (the military supplied two soldiers for taps and folding of the flag), I sensed my dad standing on the left side of the tent, in front of the line of seats where we sat. He was very pleased by the tributes. Right after Taps finished, I saw a bright white light to my right and asked my sister-in-law sitting to my right if she saw it. She didn't. Up until that day, I had never before seen the light that takes spirits to the other side. It was amazing.

I looked over and on the hill where the light was coming from, behind where the funeral home director was standing, I saw figures come into focus. From right to left were my grandmother (dad's mom) holding an infant, her second husband, and her first husband (my dad's father), then my mom's parents. Sitting in front of them were three dogs: my parent's first dog Penny, a Cocker Spaniel; their second dog, Gigi, a Poodle, and my puppy Buzz, a Weimaraner, who was killed by a car in 2005. They were waiting for my dad. I then sensed dad walking past mom and I and the others and into the light. The light was fading as the service ended and people were turning to depart. I told my mom and my partner Tom what had happened. It's something I'll never forget.

APPORTS AND ELECTRICITY

"Apport" is the action of a spirit or Earth-bound ghost to move things in a house. That's what Tom and I and my mother experienced at her house during the week of my Dad's services.

On Tuesday, before the wakes, Tom, my mom and I had put out two items in my mom's kitchen that we needed in order to do two tasks. One was a metal piece of hardware to repair the kitchen sink, and the other was a wallet with some of my dad's credit cards. When we went back later that day, both items were missing from the kitchen and there was no one else in the house all day.

On Wednesday, my mom, Tom and I had been still looking like crazy for those items. My mom asked my dad aloud to help find these things. The next day, Thursday, we walked in the kitchen, the faucet piece was back on the kitchen window, and the wallet was on the counter. There was no one else in the house.

On Friday, Tom and I were trying to help my mother with some things around the house. One thing we needed to fix was an electric outlet that suddenly stopped working Wednesday night, the day of the wake. I had a feeling that my dad was hanging around my mom's house that night (Wednesday) keeping watch over her. Usually, Earth-bound spirits that hang around affect electricity, so this was no surprise to me the outlet that mom had the coffeemaker plugged into suddenly stopped working.

The other odd electric thing that happened was that Mom's backyard floodlight suddenly went out that same night, Wednesday. Mom and Tom kept asking what was suddenly wrong with the electric things in the house. I told them how Earth-bound spirits who are hanging around (even until they pass) can affect electric things. Spirits can draw electricity to manifest themselves and sometimes short-out electric outlets or make lights flash.

On Friday, Tom and I propped a ladder against the back of the house and replaced the floodlight bulb with a brand new one. We flipped the switch, and the light didn't go on. We flipped it over and over, to no avail. Not having another new bulb, we let it go. I asked my dad for his help to make things work and thought that now that he passed into the light, he could help.

Tom dutifully then replaced the electric socket, and the plug worked. Later that night, Tom let our dogs out in Mom's fenced-in backyard and flipped the switch out of habit. The light went on. I knew my dad took care of it.

BEYOND THE SCOPE OF COINCIDENCE

In addition to my full-time job, I'm also a meteorologist, and one of my weather passions is hurricanes. Oddly enough, the very week my dad passed, Tropical Storm Edouard (Spanish for "Edward," which is my dad's name) formed in the Gulf of Mexico. Coincidence? No. In the spirit world, spirits know when they're going to pass before they're born. In fact, they know what challenges await them in the life they choose to live so that they can learn more lessons. I think that before my Dad's spirit came to Earth as a baby, he foresaw the timing of his death and the development of Tropical Storm Edouard knowing that one of his sons would grow up to be a meteorologist. Just so you know, tropical cyclones in the Atlantic and Eastern Pacific Oceans have a pre-determined six-year list of names.

PHOTO: NASA satellite image of Tropical Storm Edouard from August 4. Edouard came ashore along the Gulf Coast on August 5, 2008.
Credit: NASA

SIGNS FROM DAD, FIRST CHRISTMAS WITHOUT HIM: 2008

On December 23, 2008 when Tom and I were turning in for the night at home in Maryland, I asked my dad aloud if he'd give me a sign that he's around on Christmas. He did.

The next night, Christmas Eve, after having dinner at our house with Tom's parents, we drove to a local church Christmas concert.

During the concert I wasn't feeling the best and was slightly light-headed. It was a similar feeling I had before my friend Lynn's mother came through to me last summer. About half way through the concert, I closed my eyes and saw my Dad sitting next to a Christmas tree with my late grandmother, Dorothy (his mother) on the other side of it. Dad first appeared to me similar to the way he looked about a year or two before he passed, as did my grandmother. Then, I saw them both revert back to how they looked when they were in their 30s. This photo of my dad is from 1958 when he was around 30 years old. The vision kept flashing back and forth between how they looked just before they passed to their younger selves.

PHOTO: My dad as he appeared when he was around 30 years old. Credit: Norma G.

This isn't odd because when spirits pass, they first appear the way they did around that time, and then choose what "appearance" to have in the next realm, which is usually younger. Both my dad and my grandmother looked young and vibrant, with light brownish hair (no grey and no wrinkles). This is apparently how they choose to look in the afterlife.

The next thing I saw was my Dad standing behind my mother, who was seated in a chair facing a Christmas tree. She was wearing black and white, and I saw a flash of red.

Dad also showed me a gold decorative pin of a Christmas tree with little stones in it. He told me that this was his favorite and mom should wear it. The vision then faded.

After the concert, I called my younger brother's house, where my mom was on Christmas Eve. My sister-in-law answered. I asked her if mom was wearing black and white with red, or if she had the Christmas tree pin on. She said "no" to both. I thought, Hmmm...what was that vision about then? I said "Merry Christmas" and after hearing how my nephews liked their presents Tom and I sent them, I hung up. She didn't mention it to my mother. The next night would be confirmation of what I saw.

The next night was Christmas, of course, and after a nice Christmas dinner at home with friends, I called my mom. She had just returned home from Christmas dinner. My older brother and his wife took my mom to a relative's house for Christmas dinner.

I said to my mom, "Are you wearing black and white with some red?" She didn't answer for a minute. Then she asked "Why?" I said, "Dad told me you'd be wearing black and white today and sitting near a chair facing a Christmas tree. He showed me a little red, too. He also showed me that he was standing behind you the whole time." Mom was shocked. She was wearing black and white.

Further, she said, when she was getting dressed to go to dinner, she also took out a red blouse instead of the white one she eventually put on. She wanted to know how I knew. I told her that Dad came to me, showed the colors to me and that he was with her all day on Christmas Day. Mom and I both cried over it.

Mom wasn't wearing the Christmas tree pin, but knew where it was and would wear it on the 26th. Having this ability has been a real blessing to me and a true comfort for my mother. Honestly, it still freaks me out when I confirm things that spirits show me.

MY DAD HELPS OUT IN A PINCH

There are many benefits to being able to communicate with spirits. They can tell you things about the environment around you that you may not be aware of. During the first week of March 2009, I was home sick with the flu. The previous weekend, my partner and I were out shopping and we bought disposable razors but couldn't find them, despite emptying all of the bags from the store. We even checked my pick-up truck.

During the week that I was home sick, I decided to see if my dad could help me, so while I stood in the kitchen surrounded by our dogs, I asked my dad aloud (spirits need to hear you speak; they don't read minds) to help me find those razors.

I went back to cleaning the kitchen counter, then felt like I needed to walk into the garage (which is attached to the house and through a door that connects from the kitchen). I walked into the garage and looked around. This was a form of "inspirational thought" as described in a previous chapter.

I said out loud, "What in the world am I doing out here?" I glanced toward the tool bench and below it on one of the shelves was a white plastic bag, filled with flower bulbs that we bought the previous weekend. I walked over and picked the bag up, and there were the two packages of razors. I never would have found them out there, and I thanked my Dad aloud for his help.

DAD SAYS HELLO WHILE I WAS EDITING THIS BOOK

On July 4, 2009, when I was doing my first edit of this book, I was listening to KTHT-FM 97.1 FM online radio out of Houston, Texas. They play country oldies. Right when I reached this chapter about my dad, Holly Dunn's "Daddy's Hands" hit from the early 1980s came on. It's sung from the perspective of an adult who remembers her father's hands being gentle to hold her when she was crying, and "hard as steel" when she did wrong. The lyric says that there was always love in her daddy's hands." There is no such thing as a coincidence. This was a message from my dad, to let me know he's here. It brought tears to my eyes, and I was grateful to hear from him.

DAD HELPS ME FIND MY MOTHER'S DRIVER'S LICENSE LONG-DISTANCE

October 2009 marked a year and two months since my dad passed away. But Dad is always there when I need him, and October 13 was no different. All I had to do was call him and he was there to help.

It was 7:10 p.m. when I called my elderly mother who lives in Massachusetts. She was in a panic because she couldn't find her driver's license and was supposed to be at a function for my younger brother in the local area at 7 p.m.

When my mother panics, it's hard to get her to breathe and take a minute to collect her thoughts. I kept trying. The first time I called, she picked up a portable phone that she has in the basement of the house and told me she was in her basement searching for her license. I asked where she last saw it. She said it was in her blue jean jacket when she went for a walk the day before, but it wasn't there now. So she ran through the house frantically searching for it. The portable phone she was talking on turned off twice. I called back and told her to go upstairs, so she went into her bedroom to continue the search and pick up another portable phone located in that room.

Before I called back again, I asked my dad for help. Dad came to me and showed me the yellow kitchen benches in the upstairs kitchen, around the table. I told her to look in the kitchen around the kitchen benches (without telling her Dad's spirit told me) and she refused, saying "It's not there!"

So, I asked Dad for help again. He gave it to me. Dad then showed me mom's closets, and I told mom to go into the closet where the shoes were. Dad showed me a small white "wallet-looking thing" that had her license in it, and mom confirmed it was in that kind of a holder!

I told Mom to look around her shoes, and the bedroom remote phone shut off by itself. I called back, and the phone turned off again in less than a minute. I called a third time and in a minute it shut off again in a minute (it had a full charge on it, so said my mother). So, my Mom had no choice but to use the Kitchen phone. "Hmmm," I thought, "that's where Dad showed me her wallet/license was in the first place."

I called my mother back yet again, and she answered the kitchen phone. She then sat on the kitchen bench. She gasped. There was the wallet and the license underneath a scarf!

Of course, she started crying asking how I can communicate with Dad. I simply told her "I asked him to help and he did. Further, that was the first place he showed me to look."

So, why did my Dad take her into the bedroom? Because she refused to look in the kitchen the first time, and when she was in the bedroom, he kept turning off the phone so she'd have to use the kitchen phone. Spirits sometimes have to work really hard when someone doesn't want to listen! Thanks, Dad, I love you!

CHAPTER 11
Tom's Late Partner Visits

Tom's late partner of eight years passed away in the early morning hours of December 19, 1996. His name was Ed G. I never had the opportunity to meet Ed in this lifetime, however, I have "met" Ed through my special gift.

Ed's passing was a traumatic event in Tom's life that he will never forget. He and Ed had shared many wonderful times together; those memories and that bond didn't end with Ed's passing, they just change over time.

Tom's grandmother, someone whom I did meet before she passed in May 2006 has made many appearances to him. The following is an accounting of Ed's appearances, followed by signs from Tom's grandmother.

ED APPEARS TO ME

The first time I sensed Ed was in 2007 as we were driving back to Maryland from eastern Virginia in my extended-cab pickup truck. We had just come from Tom's grandmother's grave. I was driving, and Tom was in the passenger seat. Although I never met Ed, Tom had shown me photos of him. He was a handsome, slender young man with dark hair and a nice smile (mischievous, I would say). While driving, I looked in the rear view mirror to check traffic, and I saw Ed looking back at me. It was startling, of course. I told Tom that Ed was there with us and is watching over us.

Tom and I had been talking over the summer about finally consolidating our households. That meant selling my townhouse and moving into his house. I was ready. Tom wasn't ready at that time, which was fine, as both people in a relationship need to be comfortable. This is important because it came up later, and not by me.

CONFIRMATION OF ED'S PRESENCE FROM ANOTHER SOURCE

Later in the year, in September 2007, we received confirmation from another source that Ed was indeed watching out for Tom and was around us. We went to a psychic in old Ellicott City, Maryland. We had been there once before early in our relationship, and two different psychics that sat us in separate rooms each told us that we were the other's soul mate. This time was no different. However, this time, the psychic that met with Tom told him other interesting things. First, the psychic asked Tom if he had a previous partner that had passed. Tom said "yes." The psychic then told Tom that his late partner Ed was still around and watching over him. Further, the psychic said that Ed told the psychic Tom has found his soul mate in me. Wow.

The second thing that the psychic said was that Tom and I would move in together before the end of the year. At that time, Tom said he didn't believe it, recalling our conversation in the summer that he wasn't ready. Two months passed. During that time, we had finished most of the renovations on my townhouse (we eventually wanted to sell it, but were under no timetable). One day after work as usual Tom drove up to my townhouse for dinner (we alternated between houses for a long time); he came in the house exasperated from the traffic and said "We need to consolidate." It was the week before Thanksgiving (and his birthday). Furthermore, it was before the end of the year, as the psychic had said. Had Ed influenced all of this? I don't know for sure, but I have a strong feeling he did. Further, his telling the psychic that Tom and I are soul mates was a good confirmation, too.

ED COMES THROUGH ON THE ANNIVERSARY WEEK OF HIS PASSING

Ed didn't come to me for more than another year after seeing him in my truck in the summer of 2007. During the weekend of December 15-16, 2008 Tom and I were out Christmas shopping in Barnes and Noble. I wasn't thinking of Ed or anything other than shopping. As we came out of the store, Tom said something to me, and I suddenly heard in my head "Call him an "MOT," so I said aloud, "You M.O.T.!" Then I said "Mean 'Ole Thing." Tom stopped in his tracks and said "Who told you to call me that?" I instantly responded "Edward." Then I stopped in my tracks. Wow. Tom said that Ed always used to call him a "Mean 'Ole Thing." Ed was with us that night, being as feisty as ever. He was letting us know that he's still around 12 years after the date of his passing.

NO SUCH THING AS A COINCIDENCE: ED RESPONDS TO REQUEST

One of the things that I've learned about dealing with spirits and earth-bound ghosts is that there is no such thing as coincidence. You may think something happened that coincides with what you're doing or thinking (like a song coming over the radio right after you think about it), but it was suggested. In that case, a spirit can suggest a song to you and then it will come on the radio. Take that as a signal.

One such event happened last night, Jan. 13th, 2009 but to explain it I need to go back to the night of January 12th. On the 12th, when we were getting ready to turn in, I asked Tom if he'd like to get confirmation from his late partner Ed, that Ed is still watching out for him. Of course, Tom said "yes." So, I asked Ed aloud (spirits need to hear you communicate, they don't read minds) if he could let us know he's around.

I made the same request of my Dad on Dec. 23rd, and Dec. 24th he came to me and proved it (see Chapter 10: My Dad, about Christmas Eve, 2008). Well, last night, Jan. 13th, 2009 without even realizing it, Ed had made himself known. I was writing notes on our "newsletter" that we send out quarterly to friends around the U.S. and came across Ed's father's name. When I went to ask Tom if he wanted to write a note, I unconsciously said aloud, "Do you want to write a note to Ed G.?"

Tom looked at me. I stopped and realized that despite Ed's father's name written in front of me, I said "Ed's" name aloud. Now, granted that sounds simple, but Tom said immediately afterward, that's funny that you said Ed's name because I was just downstairs and opened a drawer and there were old photos of Ed that I had forgotten were in there.

So, although it seems like a coincidence, it's not. If you know spirits, its subtle things like that they use to communicate their presence.

CHAPTER 12
Tom's Grandmother's Passing – Many Signs

Tom hasn't had many experiences with spirits, but his grandmother has made a number of appearances to let him know she's watching out for him. Here are a couple of Tom's experiences.

ANGELIC BEING FOREWARNS OF HIS GRANDMOTHER'S PASSING

On Saturday, April 8, 2006, we visited Tom's 95-year-old grandmother at a nursing home in Colonial Beach, Virginia. She had been there since January of that year. We knew that she had cancer throughout her entire body, and doctors said that if she lasted another 2 ½ months they would have been surprised.

His grandma appeared distracted during our visit. We brought Dolly (the Weimaraner pup) and grandma didn't even pay her any attention, quite a difference from our previous visit. On that day in April, she told us that she hated being there, but knew she needed around the clock care. She said it's "for the birds." When we were leaving, Tom knelt beside her and she looked in his eyes and said, "Take care of yourself." It appeared as a final goodbye. The next day, strange things happened.

Tom wrote: *I was staying at Rob's townhouse on Sunday, April 9, 2006. I kept my clothes in a separate spare bedroom at the end of the hall. I got up at my usual time, about 5:30 a.m., and walked toward the spare room. As I looked up, in my bleary-eyed state, I witnessed the ghostly image of a woman cloaked in a long white robe that was cinched about the waist. She had long black hair but her face was obscured. The outline of the image did not resemble anyone that I recognized. As soon as I walked into the room, the image vaporized right before me. I kind of stood there for a second to take in what had just happened to me.*

I don't believe that what I saw was a vision of Grandma. What I believe is that there are "elders" on the other side – souls that help us, the living, pass on when it's our time to cross over. They make appearances to loved ones, those of us left behind, to prepare us for the imminent passing of a loved one. So I believe that I saw one of these elders.

Later that afternoon, Tom and I were working in the dining room, finishing up the wood flooring trim. I looked outside the window, and two dark shadows, that looked like birds swooped by. I didn't see any birds, just shadowy figures. I remember that my Italian mother told me that birds will fly near a window when someone is about to pass on. I'm not sure if these were spirits foretelling of Tom's grandmother's passing or not, as I didn't get a good look at them.

Tom's grandmother, Grace, passed away the next month, May 2006. It was from that time on that she started letting Tom know that she was around him and watching out for him all the time.

GRANDMA'S PENNIES FROM HEAVEN

As stated previously, one of the ways in which people who have passed into the light can communicate is by dropping small amounts of money, usually in the form of a penny, in front of those they love. Tom's grandmother, Grace, started doing that immediately after her passing and continues to do it three years later.

One time, Tom and I went to the gym together and I sat on the bench to tie my sneakers. When I picked up my sneaker, Tom saw a penny underneath it. I know for a fact that there was no penny there before I sat down. I always look down, and I didn't see anything. I know his grandmother placed it there for Tom.

Over the course of the last several years, Tom has found a lot of change. Right after grandma Grace passed, Tom was finding change a on a daily basis. Tom joked that he wished grandma would "start dropping ten dollar bills."

Here's an example. This is an email from Tom on July 9, 2008 to me.

From: W., Thomas Sent: Wed 7/09/08 6:11 AM
To: Rob Gutro
Hello Rob – You won't believe this. The office has black carpet. The housekeeping crew comes through every night to vacuum and empty the garbage cans. I came in this morning, turned down the aisle to my cube, and there on the floor was a shiny penny, heads up, right smack in the middle of the aisle with Lincoln's head pointed towards me. I said, "Thanks Grandma." She's looking out for us.

CHAPTER 13
Some of My Other Experiences

AN EARTH BOUND GHOST: MY AUNT APPEARS TO ME, NEEDING FORGIVENESS, EARTHBOUND

I had two sets of aunts and uncles, both on my mother's side. One was my mother's brother who passed away in the early 1980s, and the other was my mother's sister Romilda, also known as "Tillie," who passed away in 1983. She died suddenly of a stroke, and only my mother was at the hospital when she passed.

My mother told me many stories about how her sister, Tillie, was always causing trouble during her time among the living. Tillie stole some of my mother's clothes and other things during her lifetime. They had a love-hate relationship. Despite that, my younger brother and I would occasionally stay with my Aunt Tillie and Uncle Richard when we were kids, and we enjoyed our time together. We learned songs like Bobby Vinton's "Red Roses for a Blue Lady" and Marty Robbins' "White Sport coat and a Pink Carnation." My uncle, who passed in the 1970s, always had a fun way of accusing my younger brother of cheating at Checkers and dancing with my aunt in the kitchen. I loved both of them, and tried not to pay attention to the up-and-down relationship my aunt had with my mom.

A couple of weeks before my aunt passed away, my mother told me that Tillie had asked for forgiveness for all of the bad things she had done to my mother during their lives. My mom said, "no." I guess my mom learned about harboring grudges from her parents. My aunt passed away without being forgiven by my mother. I later learned that she didn't achieve peace because she didn't get my mother's forgiveness. It is critical that everyone forgive people before, or even after they pass, and really mean their forgiveness. Just saying it doesn't work.

When I moved to Kentucky in 1996, I wound up living in a haunted house. I didn't know it was haunted, however until after I moved into it. More on the haunted Kentucky home in Chapter 15: Experiences in Various Houses and Locations. One night in that house, I was sleeping soundly when I woke up suddenly. At the foot of my bed appeared a dark shadow in the shape of a person, just standing there. It said nothing and didn't move.

I immediately knew it was my aunt. She told me in my mind that she needed forgiveness from my mother so she could move into the light. I wondered then why I couldn't see my aunt's face, but it could be because she didn't want to be seen as she was still experiencing guilt as an Earth-bound ghost.

Spirits who feel guilt over things they've done in their life on Earth may feel they don't deserve to go into the light, so they stay behind trying to get that forgiveness. Unless they can communicate with someone who knows what they need, they can remain trapped as Earth-bound ghosts.

I shared that story with my mother in 1996. She said she wanted my Aunt's ghost to leave me alone. I told her that it doesn't work that way. If an Earth-bound ghost reveals that he or she is seeking forgiveness, they won't go away until they get it. They're bound to roam the Earth. I explained to my mother that because my aunt Tillie's ghost was able to come communicate to me she once, would be able to do it again and again until she achieves forgiveness and passes into the light.

Every now and then I would ask my mother to forgive my aunt, and I would still get the "no" answer, and "If you only knew what she did to me." In 2008, shortly after my dad passed, I brought up the subject of my aunt's ghost again to my mother. She finally said, "I forgive her if it will help her."

Since then, I haven't felt my aunt's presence, and I hope that she's finally passed into the light and into the peace she's longed for, for more than 25 years.

The lesson here is that grudges need to be released. Although it's important to do drop grudges and forgive people when they are alive, the deceased also need forgiveness to move on. It does a living person no good to maintain grudges, especially after someone has passed away.

OUR HAUNTED GUESTROOM MATTRESS

I'm also able to sense if a spirit has attached itself to a piece of furniture or a place. When I moved into Tom's house (hereafter referred to as "our house") in 2007, I immediately got an uneasy feeling upstairs. It was as if a female presence was living there.

Sometimes it's difficult to identify which object an energy may be attached to, especially when you're in a room with a number of old pieces. Such was the case in the guestroom of our house. Whenever I went into the upstairs guest room, I developed a headache in the back left part of my head. That told me there was a presence in that room.

I knew the female spirit in the room didn't want to be disturbed, so I obliged it. We could live in harmony with a ghost, but I really wanted her to pass into the light.

We always kept the door closed, and sometimes when we would try to enter (we kept all of our ties in that closet), the door would be locked from the inside! We'd try again later, and the door would easily open. There was no physical explanation for it.

Whenever I went into the room I was always drawn to the bed and the dresser. I couldn't tell which piece of furniture the ghost's energy was attached to. Tom told me that the dresser was from his great-grandmother (but I didn't sense a relative), and that the bed and the mattress were purchased from the neighbor of a friend of his in Washington, D.C.

In late 2008, we bought a new mattress for the master bedroom and swapped out the master bedroom's old mattress with the one that was in the guest room. We decided to give the guest room's original mattress away to a needy person after I convinced the ghost to pass into the light.

We posted it on Craigslist as "free," a college student requested it. When we lifted the mattress off the bed, there was a spot in the middle of it. I don't know what that was, but I got a feeling that the mysterious woman who has been locking herself in our guest room had passed away on this mattress some years ago. Before we delivered the mattress, I asked the ghost to cross into the light where she belonged. I didn't feel anything remaining in the room when we started to move the mattress out of it.

We delivered the mattress to the happy college student, who happened to be into the Goth look and was all dressed in black. We returned home to see if there were any other incidents of the door locking. There haven't been any, and I don't sense anything in that room anymore, so the ghost of the woman was obviously attached to the mattress.

I do think the older woman's ghost crossed over, but if not, she wasn't harmful so there won't be a problem with her sharing the mattress with the needy college student. Of course, the student would probably prefer a warm body instead of an icy cold ghostly one!

Before I moved into Tom's house in 2007, he had a roommate that rented the other room upstairs, located across from the guest room that once housed the ghost-attached mattress. The roommate later confirmed that he had seen the ghost of a woman walk into the hallway outside of his room one night. He couldn't explain it.

LYNN C'S MOTHER SENDS A MESSAGE TO ME IN THE OFFICE

On Friday, July 11, 2008, at around 2:15 p.m., I had just returned to my office after taking a late lunch. As I entered my office, I became light-headed and heard in my head a message from the mother of my friend and co-worker, Lynn C., who lives near Annapolis, Maryland.

Her mother told me, "Mail Lynn the postcard of the Boxer (dog) you've been holding on to," and instructed me to let her know that her mother is watching over her. Lynn and her husband and son have two Boxers, and I've had that Boxer dog post card for about 6 months and have been forgetting to mail it to Lynn. I made a note to do that.

I called Lynn immediately after that and reached her in her office. She said her mother passed a year ago that month, and July 30th would have been her mother's birthday.

Lynn was very emotional during the entire month and had previously told me that she was taking the next week off to meditate about her mother. Maybe that's why her mother came through to me that day. What was even more ironic was that Lynn said she heard from a girlfriend the day before at around the same time (2:15 p.m. ET), who also said Lynn's mother came through and told her to tell Lynn to take time off. Both I and Lynn's other friend confirmed that Lynn's mom is around her. (I'd like to know what the significance of 2:15 p.m. is; perhaps that was the time of her passing).

It is interesting how two different people who don't know each other gave Lynn the same message one day apart, around the very same time of day. This was definitely not a coincidence; it was Lynn's mother sending messages.

LYNN J'S MOTHER SENDS A RED DRESS MESSAGE

My friend Lynn J's mother passed away in 2006, and I went to the wake. While at the wake I sensed that Lynn's mother was not there, but she was in the kitchen of a house, seated with her husband (who had passed years before).

While looking around at the photos that Lynn and her family displayed, I noticed one of her mother in a red dress. Immediately, I heard her mom say "I don't like that dress, and I wish Lynn didn't put that picture out." I told Lynn, who said, "That really sounds like my mother."

CHAPTER 14
My Experience Among Strangers – My First Public Readings

On Saturday, May 2, 2009, Tom and I attended a seminar in northern Virginia called, "A Closer Look: After Death Communications." It was organized and hosted by a local spiritual theorist, lecturer and para-psychic event coordinator named Janice M. Ervin. We met Janice as a result of seeing an article on her in the local newspaper. I contacted her, and we met her and her co-event planner Deb at the local Panera Bread one evening to talk about mediumship and past life experiences. She told us about this seminar. Janice's website is *http://janiceervin.com/*.

The seminar featured Dr. R. Craig Hogan, author, researcher and lecturer, Jennifer Farmer, spiritual teacher, intuitive, and medium; and Barb Mallon, spirit medium. Each of them was fascinating, and Dr. Hogan explained how the consciousness was "outside the physical brain," among other interesting statements including scientific studies that prove metaphysical activities. Farmer and Mallon did psychic readings around the room, which were quite unnerving.

When we arrived, the hotel conference room was already nearly filled, so we sat in the last row on the left. I immediately got a headache in the back left corner of my head, which told me there were a number of spirits in the room. I knew they were spirits, though (the ones that had passed into the light and came back to give messages) and not Earth-bound ghosts. I slipped Tom a note saying, "there are a lot of spirits here wanting to talk."

CHARLIE SENDS A MESSAGE

Right after that, I heard a spirit in my head telling me things, so I wrote them on the pad of paper in front of me. He said his name was "Charlie" and there was a "W" associated with him or the person he was trying to contact. He showed me that he was about 65 when he died. He let me feel pain in the left side of my chest, which indicated to me it was a heart attack that took his life. He showed me snippets of his appearance: short, stocky, short white hair sticking up and a large nose. He showed me a blue plaid shirt. Then he showed me work boots and a truck, as if he were a truck driver. He also showed me a white dog. I couldn't tell who in the room he was trying to communicate with, so afterward I told Janice Ervin (the conference organizer) and she said she would let me talk about it at the end of the program. This was the first of two messages.

At the end of the seminar, Janice Ervin let me stand up and say all of these things out loud. Oddly enough, a 30-something-year-old woman across the aisle said, "That's my grandfather." She explained he looked just like what I described, and said that the in ONLY photo she has of him, he's wearing a plaid shirt. She also said that he died when she was six. I told her that he just wanted to let her know that he's with her and watching over her. She was amazed!

ANNA SENDS A MESSAGE

Toward the end of the seminar, medium Jennifer Farmer taught everyone how to meditate and focus. She dimmed the lights and played one of her CDs with slow breathing instructions. My mind emptied, only to be filled with thoughts from an elderly woman named "Anna." When I stopped meditating, I immediately wrote down everything Anna told me.

She was in her eighties when she died. I wrote "around 87." She showed me the years 1910-1940, indicating that she may have been born during those times. I saw a large open farmland area, with a shack of a house, "like Minnesota" I heard. She told me she was related to someone with a "G." She also said that she was the grandmother or mother of someone in the room. She said she's around this person, always watching over them. Further, she told me that the person she "belonged to" lives in a brick apartment or condominium, and she showed me a fountain, indicating there's water around it. (We were in northern Virginia, west of Washington, D.C., so there's no water nearby).

While reading what I had written to the people in the room, a woman sitting four tables up from me immediately said "Anna, that's my mother." The woman, who didn't give her name, said that her mother passed in a community that looked out over an open field and farmland in northwestern Maryland (Montgomery County). She said that she was, in fact, 83 when she passed away, which was recently. Further, the woman told me that she does live in a brick condominium, and there's a lake next to the building, confirming the water aspect. Sometimes spirits will show you something to make you think of something related. The woman was shocked. She said that she had already "tuned out" for the day, not expecting anyone to come through for her.

I was surprised and pleased that the two descriptions of spirits that came to me were so detailed, that two people immediately recognized who they were. It was a sign to me that my abilities are developing, and I was thankful that I was able to bring comfort to both of these women by letting them know their loved ones are okay and are watching over them.

CHAPTER 15
Experiences in Various Houses and Locations

Since 2005, I've been able to go into a house or a place and sense an Earth-bound ghost. Whenever there's a presence, I develop a dull headache in the back left side of my head. That's only happened since 2005, when I fell in love. Before that, spirits made themselves known to me by other means, such as appearing in a photograph when there was nothing there, or making lots of noise.

In this chapter, I'll take you on a tour of cities and places I've been where I've encountered spirits. The places include the very haunted Tombstone, Arizona; Bowling Green, Kentucky; Oella, Glenn Dale, Laurel, and Bowie, Md. and Washington, D.C.

ARIZONA

TOMBSTONE, PHOTOGRAPHED EVIL FACE IN A PAINTING
I visited Tombstone, Arizona, for the first time in the summer of 1993. It was with my friend John, after we were both inspired by the Kurt Russell/Val Kilmer movie "Tombstone." The movie was a depiction of Wyatt Earp's life in the town and became one of my favorites.

Upon visiting the town, we discovered that this once thriving silver mining town in the 1880s was a tourist town. Back in the 1880s, a miner named Ed Schieffelin went to Camp Huachuca with a band of soldiers and left the fort to prospect for silver. The story goes that soldiers in the fort told him that he'd find nothing but his own tombstone. They were wrong, however, and Schieffelin struck silver in 1877. He named his first claim the "Tombstone Silver Mine," and the town took on that name.

Tombstone was a violent town in its heyday. In fact, it's been said that there were more murders there in the 1880s than in modern day Los Angeles. A lot of violent deaths mean a lot of Earth-bound ghosts, and Tombstone has a number of them.

Of course, the event that put Tombstone on the map and in newspapers such as *the New York Times,* was the famous shootout near the O.K. Corral (not "at" the O.K. Corral, because the shootout actually happened behind it) on October 26, 1881. That shootout involved Wyatt, Virgil, and Morgan Earp and their friend Doc John Holliday against the "Cowboy gang," which included the Clantons and McLaurys, who were known cattle-rustlers, stagecoach robbers and thieves.

PHOTO: The stage and curtain inside the Bird Cage Theatre.
Photo by: Rob Gutro

By 1887, the silver mines around the town had flooded from rising underground waters and effectively closed the town down until 1929. The Bird Cage closed in 1889. In 1929, William Breakenridge, who during Wyatt Earp's time of 1882 was a Cochise County Deputy Sheriff, published a book called *Helldorado* about the conflict between the Earps and the Cowboy gang. That book generated public interest, and tourism started to bring the town back to life.

Many of the buildings built in the 1880s still stand in Tombstone, almost exactly as they were, although the businesses have changed hands many times. Some of the more famous streets include Fremont, Toughnut (also named for a silver mine), 3rd and 6th Streets. Some of the famous buildings include St. Paul's Episcopal Church, built in 1882; the Crystal Palace Saloon; the Bird Cage Theater and the *Tombstone Epitaph* building. The Epitaph is still being printed today.

The Bird Cage Theater is the place where I had my ghostly experience. The Bird Cage was preserved pretty much as it was in its heyday. For nine years in the 1880s, it was open 24 hours a day and served as a theater, gambling hall, saloon (there's a bar right as you come in the front door) and a brothel.

Historic records note 16 gun and knife fights and 26 deaths in the building. When I visited, I also noted a lot of bullet holes in the ceiling. There are reportedly up to 140 bullet holes throughout the theatre.

Some of the ghosts have been sighted near the main performing stage. In front of the stage is an orchestra pit with a grand piano. Some visitors have noted that they've sometimes heard music, a crowd of people or even laughter in the main room of the theatre. During the nine years the Bird Cage was open, performers included Josephine Marcus, who would later become Mrs. Wyatt Earp, Eddy Foy, Lotta Crabtree and more.

In the basement is an area that claims the longest running poker game in history. The game seated seven players and a dealer. The minimum buy in was $1,000.00, and the game supposedly ran 24 hours a day for 8 years, 5 months and three days!

According to Ghost Trackers.com at the web site *http://www.ghost-trackers.org/birdcage.htm*, "There is a picture of 'Fatima,' an exotic dancer of the period, inside the front doors to the right, just as you enter the building. It has been said that someone who took her picture has an evil face in it. Unfortunately, we didn't get anything in our pictures."

The Complete Book of Ghosts by Paul Roland also notes of that same painting, "A face has been seen in the large painting which hangs behind the bar."

PHOTO: The ghostly head of the old man appears in the large photo of
Fatima in the lobby of the Bird Cage Theatre.
Photo by: Rob Gutro

In 1993, I did capture the evil face in the painting, as shown in the photo shown here. If you look at the center of the painting of the lady Fatima (who was a performer during the period) you can see the shape of a face that looks like an older, bearded man. When I took the photo, I did not see the face. In fact, there was not even any light coming from the outside. I kept trying to figure out what that was in the photo. As I held onto it, the outline became clearer. I sent that photo and others I took to the Birdcage Theater owner at the time, Billy H. Jr. I'll never forget the phone call I received from him when he got the pictures. He exclaimed, "You actually photographed the ghost of the Birdcage!"

Billy also shared with me a number of his own encounters and those of others who worked there. He said that several people have reported seeing a male form on the stage. The man was likely an actor, long dead, who walks across the stage and disappears.

The Bird Cage Theatre has been the subject of a number of ghost hunting programs and has appeared on the History Channel. The SyFy Channel's "Ghost Hunters" team also visited. During their visit, they actually captured video of a power cord unwinding itself from around a clock!

KENTUCKY

BOWLING GREEN, KENTUCKY: LIVING IN A HAUNTED HOUSE

AUDITORY AND VISUAL, AND TACTILE SIGNS FROM BEYOND

I moved to Bowling Green, Kentucky, in the summer of 1996 so I could go back to school and obtain another degree- this one in meteorological technology from Western Kentucky University.

I was staying in Nashville, Tennessee, for a couple of months until I could find a job and a place to live in Bowling Green. Before I moved there, I drove up (about 90 minutes north) and checked out ads for roommates over 5 hours.

Because I was 33 at the time I didn't want to live in a dorm and couldn't afford a place on my own, so I opted for a room to rent.

I saw a handful of tiny apartments in buildings or houses that looked like they were not only built before the Civil War, but also as if some battles had been fought in them. I was pretty disgusted by the cramped, dirty places I had seen. In one place, the idea of sharing one bathroom with four guys who were 15 years younger than me, and slobs, was horrifying.

The outward appearance of many of the "homes" I visited in search of a room to rent, were not good, either. Most of them had been built in the 1800s and were now just housing for students, who obviously didn't care to keep them up. Neither did the landlords.

I found a young student named Ryan, 23, who was renting out one of two rooms in a house (he lived in the other room). Ryan was a nice, kind-hearted guy. He was shy, skinny, wore glasses and could do anything on the computer. He was a logical thinker, who some would consider a computer geek.

PHOTO: The haunted Kentucky house I lived in.
Photo by: Rob Gutro

His parents had purchased an old house a relatively short walk from the university so that his older sister (then graduated) and he could attend school without living in a dormitory. Good plan! The address was on East 11th Street, Bowling Green, KY 42101. In early July, I visited the house and met Ryan there. During the summer months, Ryan moved back home with his parents some 25 miles away and didn't stay in the house alone. Ryan only moved into the house during the school year. The house was small, but perfect in all aspects.

It was an older home, although I didn't know what year it was built. It had old "pans" built into the floors, where people would place hot coals in the wintertime for warmth and cover them with an iron grate.

Ryan told me that he wouldn't be moving in until the middle of August, when the school year started. I needed to move in near the end of July (1996). That left me alone in the house for a couple of weeks, which I thought nothing of, because at that time in my life I really couldn't sense spirits very well. Over the next couple of weeks, however, I came to know they were there.

I kept a written journal of the events that happened to me that summer, because it was my first experience living in an actual haunted house. The words that follow are directly from that journal.

The pounding on the kitchen door at the back of the house woke me out of a sound sleep and startled me. I was sleeping in one of the two bedrooms in the house, and mine had a window that faced the back yard. I looked at the digital clock on my nightstand, and it read "2:30 a.m." Immediately, a chill ran down my spine and goose bumps appeared on the skin up and down my arms. "Who in the hell could it be at this hour," I thought as I jumped out of bed.

Just then, the pounding happened again. It sounded like a fist hitting the outside of the door in the kitchen that led into the small backyard of the house. Of course, I jumped again.

I slowly walked down the short hallway through the dining room that connected to the kitchen. I stopped and glanced through the half-curtained dining room windows, where I noticed that the backyard motion light had not come on. I thought, "That's odd, because anyone standing at the back door to the kitchen would trigger that motion light." I knew that the motion light outside worked because it went on by itself the previous evening when a strong breeze from a cold front blew tree branches past it. The pounding continued.

Standing in the dining room, I was suddenly aware how cold it was in the house, despite the fact that it was nighttime at the end of July in Kentucky (which is never cold). I actually felt the cold of the hardwood floors chill the bottoms of my feet. (Knowing what I know now, the ghost was obviously in the house with me and wanted to make itself known, thus, the cold temperature in what was a hot house on a warm summer, Kentucky evening.)

I took another couple of steps across the dining room to the doorway into the kitchen, taking a deep breath, imagining that an intruder had already broken into the house and was standing in the kitchen. I reached around the corner and flipped the light switch up and the lights went on. The pounding on the door immediately stopped.

A quick glance into the tiny kitchen showed me an empty room. I was both relieved and terrified. Whoever it was ran when I turned the kitchen lights on.

The kitchen was tiny, with one counter that housed an old rusted metal sink, surrounded by cabinets. The old wooden warped cabinets (from what appeared to be the early 1900s) were still closed, as was the window over the kitchen sink. I could find no evidence of wind banging anything in the kitchen, because the window was closed.

Against the other wall of the rectangular kitchen was a natural gas stove that was once white, now yellowed with age. A Frigidaire refrigerator hummed through the days, as it did since it was considerably older than I.

I walked over to the kitchen window and peered outside into the small side yard on the right side of the house. The side yard consisted of a walkway and what was once a carriage house, then a non-functional garage. That side of the house was dimly lit by a street light on the sidewalk a good 50 feet from the kitchen window. My inspection of the outside of the house showed nothing amiss and no one outside. I immediately thought it was curious that such loud pounding noises that woke me minutes earlier apparently weren't heard by the neighbor, whose house was very close, certainly close enough to hear such a loud racket, But the neighbor's bedroom light was still off, and their house dark.

I gathered enough courage to walk to the kitchen's back door, where the pounding had come from. I pulled aside the blue curtain on the top part of the door and breathed a deep sigh of relief when I saw nothing outside. Still cold from standing only in boxer shorts and a tee shirt, sockless on the linoleum floor in the kitchen, I decided there was no one there now. I thought, "Did I imagine this?" I didn't know what to make of the entire event, but satisfied that no one was trying to break in and no one needed help, I went back to bed and slept with the light on.

As I thought about the event the next day, I found out that Bowling Green was an historic Civil War town, and most of the locals were amateur historians about the war, participated in battle re-enactments, or were just tired of hearing about it. I wondered if the Civil War had anything to do with the mysterious noises.

The next week, on the same night of the week at 2:30 a.m., there was another pounding at the back door. I jumped out of bed and looked at the clock. I then looked out the window and noticed the motion light wasn't on again. When I reached the kitchen this time, I had a better idea of what I was up against, so I reached around the corner and turned on the kitchen light. The pounding stopped.

RYAN MOVES IN – PREVIOUS HAUNTINGS REVEALED

The night that Ryan moved into the house in mid-August, we sat down and had dinner together. During the summertime, Ryan simply moved back into his parents' house about 20 miles south. They had a nice house, nice yard and all the comforts of home, and their home wasn't haunted. At dinner I asked Ryan if anything "unusual" happened around the house. I told him what happened to me that early morning in July. He sat and listened attentively, sipping from his can of Pepsi.

When I finished telling of my "encounter," he looked me in the eye and said, "I was wondering if that would happen again." I was taken aback and said "Again?" That's when he shared the story about his last roommate named Dean, who apparently couldn't wait to move out in 1995.

Ryan explained, "Dean used to be my roommate last year." He's a good guy, a football player for Western Kentucky University, and I thought he was fearless. Heck he was even on the university's wrestling team. Anyway, one night about a year ago (July 1995), Dean was here with his dog. He had a small Golden Retriever mix. Man, I loved that dog," Ryan said. I asked him to go on.

"Well it was in July, before I moved into the house for the school year. Just like this year, he was alone in the house as you were, except he had his dog.

Dean told me that he went to bed at midnight, and his dog, "Champ" was lying at the foot of his bed. Just before 2:30 a.m., Champ started barking like crazy and woke Dean up. Dean thought someone must have been outside, so he started to get out of bed, and he said, "Suddenly there was a pounding on the back door in the kitchen." That was exactly what I heard.

Ryan continued, "Dean and Champ walked over to the kitchen and turned on the light, expecting to see someone at the window of the back door, which didn't have a curtain at that time. There was no one there.

Dean told me that at first he thought it was a college kid just being obnoxious, trying to wake people up. But that thought didn't last because right then, as plain as day, the pounding of what sounded like two fists on the kitchen door happened again, and Dean saw the door shuddering!" Dean told him no one was on the other side of that door. Ryan said that the whole event "scared the crap out of him and he ran back to his room with Champ following quickly."

I asked Ryan how Dean didn't know that someone wasn't sitting on the other side of the door, on the step, banging the door. I had a feeling I knew the answer, and I heard exactly what I expected. "Because the motion light would have gone on, as it's directed to the back door," Ryan answered. "Spooky, isn't it?" I just nodded. Ryan said, "After that, Dean refused to be here alone."

Ryan told me that motion light was installed "years ago." He said, "When my folks bought the place for my sister. My sister was here one night sleeping over and heard that knocking, so my parents thought it would be a good deterrent for any would-be thieves."

I asked Ryan outright if he thought there was a ghost. Being a logical thinker, he answered, "Maybe." I asked him if there was a ghost, did he think it was someone who lived during the Civil War. "Could be," he replied. I told him that the whole town seems to be living in the Civil War and asked when the house was built. He said he didn't know, but he told me that the "heating pans and grates" in the house's floors did date back to civil war times. Ryan told me that he was really too busy to think about ghosts with all the computer programming courses he was enrolled in.

THE GHOST COMES INTO THE KITCHEN

By September, I had been fortunate enough to land a part-time television production position at the local cable company and was working part-time on-the-air on an FM country music station over the Tennessee border, outside of Nashville.

Fall weather in Kentucky is as unpredictable as a ghost's behavior. Summertime heat can drag into September, but this year, a cold and gusty northwest wind decided to end summer quickly on September 7, 1996. Temperatures outside dropped to 33 degrees Fahrenheit that September day, and the wind chills were already in the 20s. It would be colder inside the house too because that night, the ghost returned.

I came home at 6:30 p.m., washed up and changed into jeans, sneakers and a t-shirt. I was wearing a tee-shirt with the logo of the National Oceanic and Atmospheric Administration on it. That agency houses the National Weather Service. At that time I remember thinking, "Scientists aren't supposed to believe in ghosts. They're supposed to be logical thinkers." However, there's a balance between logical thinking and open-mindedness mixed with spirituality.

Ryan was eating dinner at his girlfriend's house that night, so I had the house to myself. At 7:15 p.m. I started making dinner, which as a college student consisted of tuna fish and Campbell's chicken noodle soup. I started eating and decided to get my climatology book from the bedroom, so I could read it while eating. I went into my bedroom, got the book and brought it back into the kitchen. That's when I noticed that all of the kitchen cabinet doors were opened!

I wondered if Ryan had come home and I didn't hear him, but I quickly dismissed that because I would have heard the back door and I was only out of the room a minute. I tried to reason and thought maybe the wind blew through an open window, but all the windows were closed. It wasn't scientifically possible. I shook my head, grimaced, and closed the eight cabinets.

I tried not to think about it, but the ghost wasn't just outside pounding on the back door. The ghost was in the house and had opened the cabinets!

I remembered that the soup was bubbling on the stove so I poured it into a bowl, and brought it into the dining room with my sandwich and my book. Dinner was uneventful with the exception of finally understanding how El Nino events alter the jet stream, causing floods and droughts around the world.

After I finished eating, I picked up my bowl and plate and walked back into the kitchen only to freeze in my tracks. The cabinet doors were all wide open again!

I thought "How could I not have heard that?" "More importantly, what in the hell is causing this and why today?" The wind was gusting outside, so I thought I could blame the wind, but I knew better. It was a ghost in the house.

I decided to address the problem and asked aloud in the kitchen "Okay, who in the hell are you and what do you want?" I was getting irritated. I said, "I'd like to know what you're doing here!" as I kept looking at the open cabinets. Suddenly, I heard from behind me, "I live here." It was Ryan, who just came back in the house. He scared the daylights out of me. Of course, he knew I was talking with the ghost.

I told him what happened with the cabinet doors. He asked if the outside wind could open them. I told him, "no."

THE GHOST RETURNS A FINAL TIME

It seemed like every Tuesday night at 2:30 a.m. the ghost made its presence known through pounding on the kitchen door that led to the backyard. Each time, the motion light did not go on. Each time, there was no one outside. I now know that the ghost was doing the pounding on the door from the inside of the kitchen!

The next week on Tuesday at 2:30 a.m., there was another pounding at the back door. I jumped out of bed and looked at the dark backyard, then at the clock that read 2:30 a.m. It was still pretty frightening to get startled out of a deep sleep.

Ryan was living there by then, and we bumped into each other in the tiny hallway between bedrooms. He said "Do you hear that?" I was as scared as he was, but he walked slowly behind me until we got into the kitchen. The pounding finally stopped when I reached around and turned the light switch on.

I walked over to the door and looked out. No motion light. No breeze. Nothing. The only thing that was there was a ghost with a message that I couldn't yet understand. I decided to talk to the ghost again and tell it to leave us alone. I stood at the door and shouted (yes, it was 2:35 a.m.), "This is our house. You no longer live here anymore. You're not welcome here. You need to move on."

I then went into my bedroom and grabbed a crucifix that I've had since my first communion and hung it up next to the kitchen door. I figured that God would keep us safe. Again, I didn't know how to communicate with spirits and ghosts, or understand why they were still here. I would learn that, years later.

I realized that telling the spirit to leave and that it didn't belong there was actually the right thing to do. I should have told it to look for the light and move on, and that its life was over. Looking back, I can't be sure of what sex the ghost was, but given the force of the pounding, I'm pretty confident that it was a man and likely a Civil War soldier.

When I graduated in 1997, I took a job in meteorology in northern Massachusetts, and yes, I took the crucifix. Ryan never mentioned another ghostly visit after I left. I believe that because I told the ghost that he was no longer welcome and that this was not his house anymore, he crossed into the light.

MARYLAND

BOWIE, MARYLAND: TWO YOUNG GHOSTS AT THE BELAIR MANSION

During the 2007 Christmas season, Tom and I went to historic Maryland mansions on the "2007 Christmas Candlelight tour." The first mansion we visited was the Belair Mansion located in Bowie, Maryland. It was built in circa 1745 as the Georgian plantation home of the Provincial Maryland Governor Samuel Ogle. The home is listed on the National Register of Historic Places.

PHOTO: The Belair Mansion. R.Gutro

The Belair estate is actually recognized as the only great colonial estate where race horse breeding was conducted over three centuries. The mansion and its nearby stables both serve as museums, operated by the City of Bowie.

We walked into the mansion and met the tour guide, who briefly told us about Governor Ogle and then mentioned Christmas traditions of the time. The rest of the tour was a self-guided walk through the house that was peppered with signs about horse breeding and the mansion's history.

It was on the second floor of this mansion that I sensed the presence of an infant or child in the nursery. I asked the guide who was on the second floor with us if she had any knowledge of any children that had died in the house. She thought I was out of my mind.

She sent me downstairs to a house historian, then to another guide who confirmed that one child had indeed died in the house and was buried in the backyard. After researching the house while writing this book, I learned that the little girl who is indeed buried in the cemetery at the edge of the mansion grounds is Anna Maria Ogle, who was born in 1849 and died in 1851. Little Anna Maria apparently doesn't know that she's dead. She is still running around in the mansion, spending most of the time in what was her bedroom on the second floor in the front of the house.

GLENN DALE, MARYLAND: HAUNTED HISTORIC MARIETTA HOUSE

Tom and I and his parents visited the Marietta House in Glenn Dale, Maryland, the first weekend in December 2007. The Marietta House was the plantation home of Gabriel Duvall, who was an associate justice on the Supreme Court in 1811.

PHOTO: The Marietta House.
Credit: R.Gutro

I sensed a spirit when I entered the house. As I mentioned previously, I usually get a headache in the back left side of my head when there's an Earth-bound ghost or spirit around. As we entered the house, we were ushered into a first floor dining room, and I got the sense of a ghost upstairs somewhere.

I confirmed the ghost's location when I entered the upstairs guest room. The guide explained how the room was used at the time Duvall and his family lived there. I told Tom that when I entered, I immediately felt anxious and uncomfortable. I also developed a pain in the center of my chest, like a heart attack. I sensed that the ghost was telling me how he passed (I sensed it was an older man who died in that room), from a heart ailment. Spirits or Earth-bound ghosts will convey the feelings to mediums of how they passed by "giving them" their pain. If you're a medium, you need to tell the ghost or spirit (either by thoughts or voice them) that they do not need to share that pain with you.

After the guide in that room finished her spiel, I approached her and asked if someone died in that room. She didn't know. I told her about my anxiousness, and she said she felt the same thing. She said when she left the room it disappeared, and she "didn't like that room." Neither did I. Obviously, the ghost of the man who died there was agitated because he had some unfinished business to do before a heart attack claimed his life.

When we walked out of the room, my chest pain disappeared. I went back into the room briefly to tell the guide about the chest pain and she wasn't surprised. We asked a guide in another part of the house whether a man had passed in that room where I had felt the chest pain and she confirmed that a man did indeed die in that room when Duvall owned it.

On August 29, 2009, we drove back to the mansion to get a photo of it for this book. Again, I encountered that male ghost but I was outside of the mansion. It was the same man that died of a heart attack that I sensed in 2007, because while taking the photo, the ghost came to me and made me feel that burning chest pain again. Once I took the picture of the house, and heard him in my head say, "get away from my home." Of course, after getting the picture ... I did!

LAUREL, MARYLAND: HOT AND COLD SPOTS IN THE MONTPELIER MANSION

Tom and I also visited the Montpelier Mansion in Laurel, Maryland, during the December 2007 on the Christmas Candlelight tour. As soon as I walked through the front door, I developed a headache, signaling to me that there was a presence in the house.

It was on the second floor in the master bedroom and a room across the hall, where I sensed a woman's spirit. I asked Tom if he was cold, and he was actually hot. My right side, however was freezing as there was a column of cold air next to me. He felt my right hand and acknowledged the cold.

Ghosts draw heat/energy out of the air to manifest themselves, thus lowering the temperature. The cold spot followed me into that second room, so I knew it wasn't a draft and was indeed a lady of the house checking out her guests.

OELLA, MARYLAND: HAUNTED HOUSE FOR SALE

The tiny historic mill town of Oella, Maryland, is located on the Patapsco River in western Baltimore County. It is between the larger towns of Catonsville and Ellicott City and was a 19th century village of functional workers' houses.

In June 2004, I accompanied my friend Jay and two of his friends, Nykia and Jackie, on Jay's search to buy a home.

One house in Oella that we looked at was located on a hill, far up the street from the flour mill in adjacent historic Ellicott City. The house was located on Glen Avenue. The house was originally built in 1850, but the only thing that appeared to be original and untouched was the hand laid stone fireplace. The rest of the house was remodeled around it.

PHOTO: The haunted house in Oella, Maryland.
Credit: R.Gutro

We all entered the front door of the house and were greeted by a realtor, who proudly pointed out the original stone fireplace on the first floor. She then showed us around the living room and the kitchen and pointed to the view of the "wide open back yard." Jay and Nykia decided to look at the backyard and went out the door leading to the yard.

Meanwhile, Jackie and I were still in the kitchen. The realtor came back in the kitchen, and then we talked about some of the house's features and walked back into the living room. We immediately heard footsteps walking around upstairs.

Jackie and I looked at each other, looked around and asked the realtor if Jay and Nykia went inside and upstairs from a back entrance. She looked at us wide-eyed and said, "No, they're in the back yard, and there's no one else in the house." It was haunted, and she knew it.

After Jackie and I walked outside on the deck with the realtor, Jay and Nykia entered the house. Immediately, they heard footsteps and called my name – only to learn we were outside on the deck and they were alone in the house (with the ghosts)! Needless to say, he didn't buy that place!

WALDORF, MARYLAND: A TOUCHING EXPERIENCE AT DR. MUDD'S HOUSE

Samuel A. Mudd was a Maryland physician who was accused and imprisoned for conspiring with and helping John Wilkes Booth in the assassination of President of the 16th U.S. President, Abraham Lincoln. Booth killed Lincoln at Ford's Theatre on April 14, 1865 by firing a bullet into the back of Lincoln's head. Booth, an actor and southern sympathizer, broke his left leg while fleeing the theatre. Booth met David Herold after the assassination and they fled together through southern Maryland enroute to their destination in Virginia. They stopped at Mudd's house around 4 a.m. ET on April 15 where a reluctant Dr. Mudd set, splinted and bandaged Booth's broken leg. Further, Mudd arranged for John Best, a local carpenter, to make crutches for Booth.

Henry Lowe Mudd gave his Samuel 218 acres of farmland as a wedding present, where he built a new house for Samuel.

PHOTO: Front side of the Dr. Samuel Mudd House, Waldorf, Maryland. Credit: R.Gutro

Dr. Mudd's house still stands today as a museum at 3725 Dr. Samuel Mudd Road, Waldorf, MD, 20601. Property consists of the House Museum, Gift Shop, Kitchen, Exhibit Building and some outbuildings located on 10 acres. Tours are given and there are some stories of paranormal activity.

While finalizing this book, my partner Tom and I took our friend Laureen to the Samuel Mudd House on September 6, 2009. The previous week, we had seen an episode of the SyFy Channel "Ghost Hunters" that featured their work in the Samuel Mudd House. During their investigation, they picked up an EVP or electronic voice phenomena of a man's voice saying "I am innocent." Obviously, this was Dr. Mudd letting the Ghost Hunters know that he was not a co-conspirator with John Wilkes Booth in President Lincoln's assassination. The other incredible piece of evidence the Ghost Hunters found was the shape of a hooded figure crossing in front of them on their infrared camera while they were walking around outside of one side of the Mudd House!

On September 6, when Tom, Laureen and I pulled into the driveway of the Mudd House, I instantly developed a headache. That told me there were ghosts around, and they were also outside (just as the Ghost Hunters confirmed in their investigation). I didn't sense any specific ghosts outside, so we went inside and took the tour. Our guide was an older woman named Georgiana. She was extremely knowledgeable of the history of the Mudd family and all of the artifacts in the house, and she had a good sense of humor. She would also confirm some paranormal happenings.

The tour began on the first floor of the house. We walked in the front door which opened to a small hallway. The first door on the left went into the front parlor, but we walked past that and entered the second (and last) room on the left, the dining room. Tom, Laureen and I stood at the far wall of the dining room and my back was against the wall. No one was behind me.

Meanwhile, Georgiana, our tour guide, stood in the parlor and explained that Booth came to Mudd's house at 4 a.m. on that fateful morning in a disguise, and gave a different name, explaining that he fell off his horse and broke his leg. The doctor brought him into the front parlor and set him on a couch under the front windows, where Mudd set Booth's leg.

During Georgiana's talk I whispered to the entity that I was sensing "I know you're here, please give me a sign." Moments later, I felt two fingers tap my right shoulder! I turned and looked behind me and there was a bare wall, about four inches from my back. No one was behind me. I sensed that there was a male presence there with me, and the ghost had confirmed it through tapping me. I felt it was Dr. Mudd himself. I then asked the ghost to do it again to make sure I actually felt what I did. I waited for the confirmation, but it didn't take long.

The tour guide then brought us upstairs, through a small hallway that connected to two bedrooms, the doctor's office and a door to the attic. We entered the front bedroom and learned Booth recovered in that room. I didn't feel anything there. We then moved into the hallway and I leaned against the banister that faced open air over the stairway that we climbed to the second floor. It was there that I received the second sign by way of a tap once in the middle of my back!

The confirmation of tactile experiences in the house came immediately. When Georgiana took us into the second bedroom she asked "Has anyone been touched on the hand, here?" I told her about being touched on the shoulder on the first floor, and again being touched in the center of my back in the hallway. She said it has occurred numerous times in the house. In fact, she said that in that hallway where I was tapped, another tour guide was explaining about the house when the nearby door to the attic swung open and the guide felt a burst of cold air sweep past him. It was obviously a ghost, between the action of opening door and the cold air (ghosts draw heat and energy out of the atmosphere to manifest themselves).

The last room upstairs that we entered was the small doctor's office. I took five steps inside the office and was at the doctor's desk next to a window facing the back of the house. There, I was touched on the elbow! When I walked back into the hallway, Georgiana asked me if I was touched again, and I told her I was touched on the elbow!

We then exited the house and walked around the backyard, where Dr. Mudd's tombstone was located in a small wooden shed. However, I didn't sense any ghosts in the backyard, nor did I receive any further touches before we departed.

WASHINGTON, DC: HANK AND RICK'S HOUSE-GHOST

Soon after Tom and I met, I was introduced to two of his oldest friends, Hank and Rick. Both are retired, and they live in a beautiful old home in the Mount Pleasant area of Washington, D.C. Their house dates back to the late 1800s and has three floors.

The day that I walked into their home for the first time, I developed a headache in the back of my head quickly. I knew that they weren't living there alone. I sensed that, on the second and third floors, there was a female presence dwelling there. I didn't mention it to Tom until after we had left.

The next time we visited, Tom mentioned to Hank and Rick that I sensed a female ghost upstairs. They were not surprised. In fact, they said that friends who have stayed over reported seeing a female ghost on the second floor. So, we climbed the stairs. They took us up to the third floor first and brought us into a front parlor with a nice window view of the tree-lined street. In the room there was a beautiful fireplace. They told us that one of the previous owners was a woman, who was cleaning out her fireplace in that room. When she started cleaning it, she was attacked by wasps that were nesting in the fireplace. She was apparently stung many, many times. They were unsure if she died in the house; however, even if she didn't, I knew she still lingered there. After all, it was her house.

They next took us down to the second floor where her ghost was reportedly seen by some of their other friends. We went into another parlor, directly below the one on the third floor. I stood in the doorway, and it was there that I felt her presence. My left arm became very cold, so I knew she was standing next to me.

As I mentioned before, ghosts need energy, which they get that from drawing heat out of the atmosphere, thereby lowering the temperature and creating a "cold spot."

When we left Hank and Rick's house that evening and drove by a group of row homes, I immediately knew which of the other houses in that neighborhood had guests of the ghostly kind residing in them. To this day, I get the same strong feelings every time driving by certain houses.

CHAPTER 16
Ghost Walks in Various Cities

One way for people to experience ghosts is by taking "ghost walks." I've been to numerous cities and experienced ghost walks, and although most had legitimate stories, some did not. It's a matter of weeding out the real stories versus the tales. Two of the most unnerving ghost walks I've been on were hosted in Savannah, Georgia, and New Orleans, Louisiana. Both are haunted places. The ghost walks are alphabetized by city: Annapolis, and Ellicott City, Maryland; New Orleans, Louisiana; San Francisco, California; and Savannah, Georgia.

ANNAPOLIS, MARYLAND

On Saturday, July 26, 2008, my partner and I took the Annapolis, Maryland Ghost Walk. Annapolis is the state capital and used to be called "Queen Anne." It was actually founded in 1708, before the United States became independent of England. Back then, the city was walled off by a high fence, and livestock would run free. People would empty their "night dirt" or human waste out of their windows and into the street below citizens were struggling to make a living as the town came into being.

There was a jail in the town, which was part of the building that now houses the Armadillo restaurant. Behind the jail is said to have been a gallows, where many lost their lives. Annapolis also had its share of witches, according to historical records, and several women were hung either in the town or on ships that left the town's port.

THE PHOTOGRAPH OF THE GHOSTLY ORB OVER THE PACA HOUSE

We stopped at one house called the Paca House, located at 186 Prince George Street, Annapolis. It was about 9 p.m. and cool Chesapeake Bay breezes were rustling the trees, but the sky was clear and starlit. Our tour guide proceeded to tell us the history of the house and its former owners.

Beverly Litsinger of the Maryland Ghost and Spirit Association provided the historic details of the Paca House, Beverly wrote in an email to me in July, 2008: *The William Paca House is located on Prince George Street. The William Paca Mansion was built between 1763 and 1765. The house is a Georgian mansion that was built as a town house. William Paca was born on October 31, 1740 and he died in 1799. He was the second son of John Paca. His father owned a very large estate in Harford County.*

William Paca went to college in Philadelphia. He graduated from College in 1750. He became a lawyer and worked for the law office of Stephen Bradley. He received his law licensed 1761 and was admitted to the bar 1764.

The political career of Mr. Paca was successful. He was appointed to represent his county in the legislature in 1771. Paca was appointed chief justice of the Supreme Court in 1778. In 1780, he became chief judge of the count of appeals. In 1782, Paca was elected to the chief magistracy in 1782. President Washington appointment him the judge of the district court of the United Sates in 1789. He served in this position until 1799. Paca married twice, the first time to a daughter of Samuel Chew, in the year 1761. The second marriage was in 1777. He married a daughter of a man from Philadelphia named Harrison. He had five children with his first wife and a son by his second wife. William Paca also signed the Declaration of Independence.

People believe the William Paca house is still haunted by William Paca. His ghostly apparition has been seen in the house standing on the staircase looking down. He appears to be standing guard protecting his home. Sometime he does not look pleased when people are touring his home. Sibyl Walski told me the story about this haunting. Another ghost that is haunting the house is known as the Rose Lady.

According to the Web site Hometownannapolis.com, the Paca house is still furnished with antiques. Changing exhibits highlight different aspects of everyday life in the 1760s and 1770s for William Paca, his wife, Mary and other members of their household.

In 1901, the Annapolis Hotel Corporation purchased the property to build Carvel Hall Hotel. The 200-room hotel covered the entire site for more than half a century. In 1965, Historic Annapolis Foundation saved this landmark, guiding the rebuilding of the garden through extensive archaeological research, and returning the house to its 18th-century appearance. It opened to the public in 1973.

As usually happens when I'm near spirits, I get a headache in the back left part of my head, and it happened when we got to the front of the house. The tour, however, did not take people in the house, it just stopped outside and where the tour guide told the stories.

I was drawn to the third floor window on the right corner and side of the house (looking at the house from the street, the window was to my right). The headache still pounded. Remembering what I learned on the New Orleans ghost tour, that if you snap multiple digital pictures of the same area, sometimes an orb (a ghostly round ball of energy) would appear so I snapped away. An orb did appear in one of several photos that I took that night.

Pictured here are before and after shots of the same spot on the Paca House's roof. This first photo shows just the blackness of the night sky. An orb did appear in the second photo, but not in a third photo taken right after it.

There is no orb in the photo, and if there were dust on the lens it would have shown up in this and all of the other photos.
Credit: R.Gutro

The second photo taken immediately after the first captured an orb, just over that third floor window. Once the photo was enlarged it was easier to see the orb. See photo below.
Credit: R.Gutro

This is the portion of the second photo, zoomed in where the orb was over the right hand corner of the roof. Note that orbs sometimes have different colors in them, as this one does.
Credit: R. Gutro

The third photo taken immediately after the other two simply showed a pitch black sky. The orb had disappeared. So, the next time you're outside a house that is known to be haunted, snap multiple photos and see if you get any orbs. I've tested and proven the theory in both Annapolis, Maryland, and New Orleans, Louisiana.

ELLICOTT CITY, MARYLAND

Old Ellicott City, Maryland, is one of our favorite places to visit. It's located about 20 minutes southwest of Baltimore City and has a lot of charm. The small "Old Ellicott City" area was founded in 1772; it's a small one-street downtown area with historic buildings lining the road. All of the buildings now house little shops: antique stores, coffee shops, elegant restaurants and more. When you walk through the town, you feel as if you're walking back in time.

Whenever I've walked through the town, however, I knew that I wasn't walking alone. Not only are there a lot of living tourists there, but there are also a lot of ghosts that haven't left. That's likely why Ellicott City has one of the most successful ghost tours in Maryland. There are a lot of stories and a lot of sightings.

Ellicott City is an unincorporated community in Howard County. It is the county seat. The town includes the first passenger railroad station in the United States, now called the Baltimore and Ohio Railroad Station Museum. It was originally built in 1830.

The town was founded in 1772 when three brothers with the last name "Ellicott" came down from Pennsylvania and decided to settle in the area. Andrew, Joseph and John Ellicott were Quakers who had grown up in Bucks County, Pennsylvania, as the sons of Englishman Andrew Ellicott. When the boys arrived in Ellicott City, they started mills around the area, one of which still stands near the border of the town of Oella.

Some of the tracts of land the Ellicott brothers bought spanned both sides of the Patapsco River. The river was necessary to power the water wheels that enabled the mills to work. They milled flour, constructed machine shops, and experimented in farming and technology. They also brought in teachers, built a Quaker meeting house and built their own houses out of stone.

The granite quarries that lined the Patapsco River provided the construction material for many of the buildings in the town as well as the curbings and walls. The blocks for the railroad were also taken from the quarries.

We've taken "Ye Haunted History of Olde Ellicott City Ghost Tour" several times, and I could recite many of the stories. Howard County Tourism runs the tours that include stories about ghostly happenings from local retailers, restaurant owners and residents.

There are quite a number of ghosts that haunt the town. One of the reasons that the town is so haunted is that the Patapsco River runs through it. As I mentioned previously, water powers ghosts and enables them to thrive and communicate.

I've had several encounters in Ellicott City. On June 28, 2008 I encountered two spirits in a retail store. Tom and I joined two friends in historic Ellicott City and walked in and out of shops before going on the ghost walk that night.

GHOSTS ATTACHED TO GOODS

One of the shops we entered was called "Joan and Eve," located near the railroad bridge and across the street from the Patapsco River. The shop was divided into three sections. The front door was in the center section, and there was a left and a right side of the shop. All sections were filled with "vintage" furniture, clothing and goods from the past.

We entered through the middle section and walked into the right side room. It was there that I sensed a ghost attached to a dresser. The ghost's presence was strong and I think it didn't want its dresser sold. I then walked into the middle section (where we entered), and the headache that usually indicates the presence of a ghost or spirit faded. Upon entering the left room, there was another spirit in there. I'm unsure if it was attached to an item or was living in the building beforehand.

GHOSTLY DOOR PLAYING

On Labor Day weekend in September, 2003 my friends Mark and David arrived from Atlanta. Because it was a Monday and we missed the ghost tours which were given only on Friday and Saturday nights, I gave Mark and David a personal haunted walking tour through downtown Old Ellicott City.

I told them about all the ghosts that are reported to haunt various buildings. We stopped at one old abandoned brick building, and I told them that the Howard County tour guide mentioned that the building hadn't been rented in 50 years, because of a screaming young female ghost named Cecilia that haunts it.

Apparently, the last time a business rented it, Cecilia made her appearance. The building's last tenant was a beauty salon. The tour guide said that back in the 1960s when it was rented, women were sitting on the first floor getting their hair done when Cecilia's ghost came descending from the second floor telling them to get out. They did, and the building sat dormant for decades.

Outside the front door of the building that night in September, 2003 I told Mark and David that story. Mark reached for the wrought iron door (installed in front of the hardwood door) on the building's front entrance and opened it. He closed it, and it opened back up! He tried closing it a second time and it opened again! Finally, he managed to close it and it stayed closed. We immediately walked away from the building very quickly. Obviously, Cecilia still wanted to be left alone.

NEW ORLEANS, LOUISIANA

On May 24, 2005, I visited New Orleans for a work-related event and signed up for one of the night-time Ghost Tours.

Ironically, two months later Hurricane Katrina would kill more than 1,800 people in Florida, Louisiana and Mississippi. It would become one of the deadliest hurricanes to hit the U.S. mainland.

According to the National Hurricane Center, Hurricane Katrina made its second landfall at 6:10 a.m. CDT on August 29 as a Category 3 hurricane with sustained winds of 125 mph near Buras-Triumph, Louisiana. At landfall, hurricane-force winds extended outward 120 miles from the center. On August 29, Katrina's storm surge caused 53 different levee breaches in greater New Orleans submerging eighty percent of the city, killing more than 1,000 in New Orleans alone.

I'm sure that there are still a number of Earth-bound ghosts who lost their lives suddenly and tragically in Hurricane Katrina that are still walking around New Orleans today. One day, I'll return to the city and hope that all of those who died in that tragedy managed to cross over.

PHOTO OF GHOSTLY ORB ABOVE A HOUSE

Before Hurricane Katrina struck, New Orleans already had a lot of known haunted places and there are ghost tours that point them out.

During the ghost walk that I took, the guide pointed to a three-level old townhouse in the French Quarter. He told of a story of a Mulato woman who lived with and was in love with a Caucasian merchant. During the 1800s, because of the foolish "societal rules" of the time, if the man married the woman, people would look down upon him and boycott his business, leading him to financial ruin. One December night, the woman was reaching her breaking point in the relationship and begged the man to marry her. The man jokingly told her that if she removed her clothes and sat on the roof in the snow and sleet, he would indeed marry her. She thought he was serious.

Our tour guide said, "At that time, the doorbell rang, and the man ran downstairs and wound up entertaining his friends for hours. He returned to the bedroom to find it empty. He checked the window to the roof and saw the woman naked and frozen to death." She still haunts the roof where she froze to death outside.

PHOTO: Note the white ball of light over the top right hand side of the building's roof. This only appeared in a couple of different pictures.
Credit: R.Gutro

The tour guide explained that if people had digital cameras and took multiple pictures over the roof of that house, they may see in a couple of them "floating orbs of energy." Several people took pictures, and sure enough, the white orbs were there. When one looked at the roof, there was nothing but pitch black night sky. The guide went on to say that the woman's energy still remains on the roof, and that on the anniversary of the night she died in December, her full figure can be seen on the roof. Several years before, in the early 2000s, a Mardi gras visitor even called the police to get a "girl" down safely from the roof.

There was no girl, simply the ghostly form of the woman who never obtained the love she was seeking.

SAN FRANCISCO, CALIFORNIA

In San Francisco on Monday, February 17, 2003, my friend Dale and I took a walking ghost tour and had an experience of our own. The "San Francisco Ghost Hunt" meets in the lobby of the beautiful Queen Anne Hotel, 1590 Sutter Street, corner of Sutter and Octavia, six nights a week at 7:00 p.m.

The ghost walk starts within the Queen Anne Hotel. From the hotel, the walk proceeds outside for a mile in a safe, quiet neighborhood on tree-lined streets in the Pacific Heights area. It took about two hours and was a great way to learn about ghosts as well as the history of the area, and to see the neighborhood.

The Queen Anne Hotel was built in the 1800s and was originally a girls' school. While we were waiting in the lobby for the tour guide, I noted that the building and the decor were old and smelled musty. There were furniture and draperies still hanging from the period in which it was built.

MARY GIVES ME A COLD CHILL

The first stop on the tour was the fourth floor of the Queen Anne Hotel. We went upstairs and entered room 410. That room was the office of Mary Lake, the principal of the girl's school in the 1890s. Mary's school taught the "art of being a lady in San Francisco during the 1890s." The tour guide went on to explain that that room 410 was the most haunted room in the hotel. The guide said that Mary died a few years after she had established the school. He said that guests in that room are awakened at night as the bed gets made up while they're sleeping in it! Also, sometimes guests find extra blankets have been placed on the bed when people are sleeping in it.

The tour guide proceeded to talk about the history of the girls' school while my friend Dale and I were standing in the room about a foot apart, facing each other. At the same time, we both felt an ice-cold blast of air brush by our opposite cheeks. I also got chills up the back of my spine. We immediately looked at each other and asked if the other felt that. We confirmed that we each felt the cold. Mary had walked between Dale and me!

Almost as if on cue, the guide walked up to us and said, "Mary is also often detected in this room as a cold spot, about right here." After the tour guide led people out of the room, Dale and I cornered the guide and told him we both felt the cold spot, as if a cold figure walked right between us. The guide said "That's what people have told me before."

Later on the ghost tour when we were out walking through the Pacific Heights neighborhood and listening to stories from the guide, Dale had a visual experience. The tour stopped in front of a house where a woman was brutally stabbed to death by her first cousin, with whom she had a secret affair. It was the cousin's way of keeping his affair permanently secret, apparently.

While listening to the guide tell the story, Dale noticed a light in the blackened/dark part of the house just before the guide mentioned that previous people on previous tours had also reported a light in the darkened windows.

SAVANNAH, GEORGIA

Savannah truly is a "City of the Dead." We visited the city in mid-February 2009 and there was a lot of activity, both from the living and the dead. The Spanish moss that hangs off the trees in the town makes for an eerie setting as the sun goes down, like ghostly fingers hanging from the sky.

We stayed in the historic district for several days, and that area has a large "dead history." There were many deaths from the Civil War and from a yellow fever outbreak in the early 1800s. So many people died, in fact, that they were buried in trenches throughout the city, and buildings were built over them.

There's a lot of ghostly unrest here, as some of the yellow fever victims were even buried alive because the disease would affect the respiratory system and put people in a coma. The fever also shut down the kidney and liver and turned the victim's skin yellow, thus the name.

After a couple of incidents where it was discovered that people who weren't dead, but actually in a coma, were accidentally buried, people started burying their dead with ropes attached to bells that were mounted on a stick above the surface. The rope led into the coffin. If the person buried awoke and rang the bell, they would be dug up, if lucky enough to last that long. That's where "dead ringer" comes from, we've been told.

HISTORY OF THE CITY OF THE DEAD

The city of Savannah is literally built on its dead. According to tour guides, there were cemeteries built on the edge of the original settlement of the town. As the original colony grew larger and developed into a port city, the cemeteries disappeared under homes and businesses that were built on top of them. Some of the dead were moved: some probably weren't.

According to our tour guide, before the first settlers arrived in Savannah, the historic area was known to the Creek and Choctaw peoples as "Yamacraw Bluffs," and it was likely a burial ground. We learned that Native Americans built their towns around burial grounds.

According to "*Ourgeorgiahistory.com*," James Edward Oglethorpe of England, together with Lord Percival and 19 other men, created a charter for what would become the state of Georgia, the new colony (in honor of King George II). All of the land between the Altamaha and Savannah Rivers, and from the headwaters of these rivers to the South Seas were included in the grant. Oglethorpe used his connections to move the Charter for the colony of Georgia quickly to the king, who signed it on June 9, 1732. By January 1733, Oglethorpe and a group of militia arrived at present-day Savannah. Oglethorpe liked the area because the Yamacraw Bluff provided protection against an assault from the river, and the swamp areas surrounding it also added protection.

Once the colony was founded and grew, more people were born and died, so burial places were created. Once the yellow fever epidemic hit the area in the 1820s, victims were filling up the cemeteries. From 1750 until 1853, Colonial Cemetery was known as the main cemetery in Savannah. Colonial Cemetery is the resting place of patriots, merchants, the state's first newspaper publisher and members of the First Continental Congress. Once filled, other places had to be established for burial of yellow fever victims.

According to visit-historic-savannah.com, the first the deaths from yellow fever were recorded in May 1820. By December 1820, more than one-tenth of the city's population died from the fever (666 people). Between 1807 and 1820, more than 4000 people died from the fever. Robert Edgerly's book, *Savannah Hauntings*, says there were two more big epidemics of the fever afterward, in both 1854 and 1876 taking thousands of lives.

MY ENCOUNTERS: ON AND OFF OF THE GHOST TOURS

Wherever we went in Savannah, there were ghosts. Not spirits, but Earth-bound ghosts. We scoured the streets and the historic district; even just going into shops and restaurants I found Earth-bound ghosts.

Fortunately, historic Savannah's streets are built in a grid format making it easy to walk anywhere. It's also pretty safe to walk around as long as you're in by midnight. There are about 23 "squares" within the grid. A "square" is a green area with houses surrounding them. They're filled with "live oak" trees (the name of the tree) that harbor "Spanish moss" that hangs from their trees. Oddly, it is neither Spanish, nor moss. It's a member of the pineapple family that propagates airborne. It was named "Spanish" after the long beards of the Spaniards that once roamed the area and "moss" because it resembles a moss. It's also loaded with chiggers, or little bugs, so it's best left alone.

My ghostly encounters that were not on any tour started with the River House Tavern, located on River Street, facing the Savannah River.

GHOST AT THE BAR

In the River House located at 125 West River Street, I was confronted with an inebriated ghost.

This restaurant is located in an 1850's King Cotton Warehouse. It faces the Savannah River and features local seafood, homemade breads and desserts, baked on the premises. We went for the desserts, and they were very tasty. After we finished dessert, I got up and headed to the restroom. As I walked by the small bar (next to the restroom), I got the telltale headache in the back left part of my head - which indicates a ghost is around. I suddenly got very woozy and felt as if I were drunk!

I made it into the men's room and fell against the wall! The ghost, who was a man, conveyed to me that he became drunk or sick and died in that building. I was able to shake it off and walk back to the table. We promptly left and my head cleared. As mentioned, ghosts will sometimes share their symptoms of how they felt just before they died, as this one did.

GHOST IN THE ART GALLERY

The City Market was another area we walked through. It is located in the northern area of historic Savannah. It's about 2 or 3 blocks south of the Savannah River. In the City Market were all kinds of shops, including many art galleries. One of the shops called "The Gallery," sold paintings from local artists and is one of about 100 galleries around the historic district. It's a huge art town.

Tom and I went in and looked around. Then we went into the gallery's basement. I immediately got a headache and sensed a male presence down there. It was not happy. I believe he was one of the victims of the yellow fever epidemic. So many people are buried everywhere around the city that you're likely standing on someone's remains wherever you go (a tour guide told us).

I was very uneasy there and felt that the ghost was angry that he died (and likely was buried while he was still alive, as some were by accident). I told the ghost to move on and look for a light in a funeral home, but couldn't gauge whether or not he listened. Regardless, I wonder if the employees know about their male basement dweller.

If they find anything amiss when they open in the mornings, such as unlocked doors or lights on that were turned off, perhaps they already know.

A SWEET-TOOTHED GHOST?

I encountered another Earth-bound ghost while shopping at the Savannah Candy Kitchen, 225 East River Street. This shop was filled with lots of homemade and tasty candies.

When I was at the back of the store (I'm unsure what it was originally), a ghost passed me and let me know that we were not alone there. I didn't stay in the store long enough to figure out if it was male or female or how that person died. I was really more interested in getting some candy, selfish as that was!

GHOSTS ON TOURS: THE SORRELL-WEED HOUSE

"Ghost on Tours" isn't the name of a tour we took; these are stories I had of ghosts that I encountered (for the most part), on the Ghost Tour we took, or in the two mansions we visited. This is all about the Sorrell-Weed House. Spirits who are believed to haunt the house include a former slave who died at the house and Francis Sorrell's wife who killed herself by jumping from a second floor balcony. I think there may be one more spirit in there.

The Sorrell-Weed house was one of the three mansions we toured. It's located on 6 West Harris Street in Savannah and was built in 1840 by General Gilbert Moxley Sorrel (youngest general in the confederate army).

General Robert E. Lee (1862) and General William T. Sherman (1864) also visited the home. In 2008, the new owner found a box inside a false ceiling that had authentic first drafts of the original surrender papers signed by General Lee.

THE GHOSTS - There are apparently a couple of them in the Sorrell-Weed House, and the house is known for them The SyFy Channel show "Ghost Hunters" was filmed there in 2005 and confirmed some entities using scientific equipment. Hosts Jason and Grant declared that the house was indeed haunted. During their investigation they captured an EVP (electronic voice phenomena) of a woman yelling, "Get out, get out... help me, my God, my God." In fact, it is now listed as Savannah's most haunted house.

MY EXPERIENCES: THE HAUNTED WAITING ROOM

Once we entered the house, we were led into the front right room until others came in. While we were there, I got the sense that we were joined by a male ghost. My headache started. While our friends were talking with Tom, I sensed our ghost had taken a seat in the rear corner of the room. I know it was a man from the 1800s. I wish I could see ghosts' images all the time, but I can't. I took a photo of the chair where the ghost was sitting. Then he moved to the fireplace.

PHOTO: The basement of the Sorrell-Weed House, where the "Ghost Hunters" TV hosts confirmed EVPs of a woman's voice.
Credit: R.Gutro

THE HAUNTED BASEMENT

When we started the tour of the Sorrell-Weed House, I was immediately drawn to the basement, for some reason. I kept looking at the stairway that led down there while the young female tour guide was showing us the first floor of the house. Once we did go downstairs, she told us that it was there in the basement that the "Ghost Hunters" confirmed spirit activity.

SITE OF A WOMAN'S SUICIDE

Francis Sorrell's wife killed herself by jumping from a second floor balcony onto a brick patio in the backyard. When the tour guide took us out there and showed us the spot, I didn't feel the presence of a ghost there in the courtyard, however. Why? Because the ghost is likely haunting the inside of the house where she was more comfortable during her lifetime. Ghosts necessarily linger around the spot they died. Mrs. Sorrell's bedroom was in a second or third story of the house that was closed off to tours, because it's still being renovated. I'm sure that is where her ghost dwells. The last two houses that we went to in Savannah had one haunting each that I was able to detect. Of course, I didn't go through one of them entirely.

THE GREEN-MELDRIM HOUSE

This house was designed by New York architect John Norris and built in 1850 for cotton merchant Charles Green. This Gothic-revival mansion cost $90,000 to build. General Sherman lived here after taking over the city in 1864 and was welcomed by Mr. Green. The house was bought in 1892 by Judge Peter Meldrim, thus "Green-Meldrim." His heirs sold it to St. John's Episcopal Church to use as a parish house.

This house wasn't on the "haunted" list, but when we toured it for its history, I sensed a ghost. It wasn't until we got into the dining room at the back of the house, that I got a headache, became nauseous and sensed a female ghost. I sensed that she didn't want people in her house. I believe this was the wife of Charles Green.

YE OLDE PINK HOUSE- MAN IN THE HOUSE

James Habersham Jr., one of the wealthiest Americans of his time, built "Ye Olde Pink House" in 1771. He became a hero during the Revolutionary War and rose to the rank of major in the colonial army.

The house was made of red bricks, covered over with white plaster. The house appears pink because the red bricks bled through the plaster.

The house has chandeliers, antiques and even original Georgia pine floors in its tavern, which is in the back left side of the house. That's where ghosts of young African-American children are known to romp. We didn't go back there, however. Of course, I didn't need to go there to sense a ghost. As soon as we came through the front door and walked up the stairway to the second floor, I sensed a man - whom I believe was Mr. Habersham. I later read that he's been seen on the second floor many times. Once we walked through the long hallway and into a huge room where we dined, I didn't sense him anymore. It turns out, we walked into a new building that was built in the last couple of years and attached to the house to expand the dining area.

THE SAVANNAH WALKING GHOST TOUR

We took a Walking Ghost Tour in Savannah called the "Sixth Sense Tour" on Friday the 13th, 2009- which we thought appropriate! It was 7:30 p.m. and dark, and perfect. I didn't sense any ghosts on the tour, only because the ghosts were in the houses that we walked past. There are some interesting stories, though, and following are a couple of them.

MERCER HOUSE

The Mercer House, located at 429 Bull Street, Monterey Square, Savannah, Georgia 31401 has a number of ghosts in it. It was designed in 1860 by New York architect John Norris for General Hugh Mercer, the great grandfather of Johnny Mercer. The Mercers never actually lived in this house. It wasn't completed until 1868. General Mercer sold the house unfinished in 1865.

In 1913, it was the home of a physician, who is said to have been pushed off a balcony, where he broke his neck on the sidewalk below.

Our tour guide said that the source of the ghost who pushed the physician is unknown. Whatever it was, it caused a lot more unrest.

The home would later be owned by famous antique philanthropist James Williams, who shot his lover, Danny Hansford, in the 1970s, and after four trials was acquitted. All this was made famous (or infamous) in the book, *Midnight in the Garden of Good and Evil*. When Williams was finally acquitted, he returned home after being in prison 9 years, and after only 6 months, died in the house of a heart attack at age 59.

After Williams died, a little boy and his friend were playing on the mansion's roof (how they got up there, only they know). The little boy was apparently pushed by the same ghost that killed the doctor in 1913. According to the other boy, he saw the boy being pushed, but he was frozen and couldn't move as the other boy fell off the roof. That boy was impaled on the fence and died. The broken arrow on the fence still remains today, and the guide told us that people often see the boy running down the sidewalk saying, "I need to go home." He didn't show the night we were there.

432 ABERCORN STREET- THE GHOSTLY FACE ON A BUILDING

This was by far the most frightening story and house on our ghost walk. In the 1800s, an Army General named Wilson lived here with his 9-year-old daughter. Because the family was "upper class," the little girl was not allowed to associate with school children of lower class that just happened to play outside of their home. There was a school for lower class children diagonally from the Wilson house, and the kids would go out in the grassy square and play at recess and during the summertime. Wilson's little girl would sit in her second floor bedroom window and beg her father to let her go out to play with the other kids. She didn't care about "classes." She was only nine. Her father refused.

One day, she ran outside and played anyway. It was a fatal mistake. Her brutally mean father actually tied her up in a chair in her bedroom and faced her toward the window to watch the other kids play.

He left her there for two days... and it was the summertime. Summer in Savannah means 99°F with 100 percent humidity. The little girl was dead of heatstroke when her evil father found her, still tied to the chair.

The general was distraught and angry after the girl's death. You can guess he was the type of person that blamed the children for his daughter's death, and not himself. After she was buried, he would sit in her chair staring out at the children. Our tour guide said he died there, too, but as an old man. I gather that he is apparently still angry and needs forgiveness for killing his daughter before he can move on.

PHOTO: Close up of general's face on the side of the house at 432 Abercorn Street.
Credit: R.Gutro

Strangely, his face has appeared on the outside of the house. His visage is seen to the left of a window on the front of the house. The Georgia Paranormal Society compared the image to photos of the general and they match. Further, one man tried moving into the house and renovating it. Workers refused to work and some ran out, leaving tools behind (which can be seen in the windows). The man who moved in was pushed down the stairs and into the front doors after he distinctly heard a man's voice say, "Get out!" He did and no one has returned in years.

Other tours I've attended and recommend include Baltimore's Fells Point Ghost Tour, the Ellicott City, Maryland, Ghost Tour; and the Harper's Ferry, West Virginia Ghost Tour. Each of these tours has fascinating stories that will make you look into the windows of old buildings and wonder if there's a pair of dead eyes looking back.

CHAPTER 17
Dogs and Cats DO go to Heaven: My Dog Buzz-Wyatt's Presence

Humans aren't the only beings who let you know that they're still around or come back and visit after passing away. Animals have the same ability, as I learned after the tragic loss of my beloved 6-month-old puppy Buzz Wyatt.

Some pets, such as dogs, cats and horses, stay true to their masters even after they pass. Some have been noted to stay behind and remind their owners that they're still around. Perhaps they're waiting for their masters to join them so they can walk into the light together. It's hard to say, but it seems logical. Others will pass into the light if someone they know has passed previously and can call them.

Some "religious" preachers, such as the one who told my friend Sandra's eight- year-old son in Alabama, that his dog would never be in heaven, because "dogs don't have souls," should be thrown out of whatever church they're in. This so-called "man of God" destroyed this little eight-year-old's hopes that he would one day meet one of his beloved canine friends in the afterlife. In my opinion, people who don't know anything about the afterlife shouldn't be teaching others about it.

I know personally that dogs, cats and other pets go to heaven. I've seen them and they've communicated with me. Mediums such as James Van Praagh, Concetta Bertoldi, and Barbara Mallon among others, have also communicated with pets on the other side.

Dogs have the intelligence of 2-to-4 year old humans, according to Stanley Cowen's book, *How Dogs Think*. Dogs also have a wide range of emotions just like people. Like children, dogs are the living embodiment of unconditional love. Dogs are innocent beings with souls, and they certainly do cross into the light.

As I wrote in Chapter 10: My Dad, I watched my Dad pass into the light at the cemetery. Standing and waiting on the other side, in the light, was my puppy Buzz Wyatt and two dogs (who had passed) that my family had while I was a boy.

In September, 2009, I spoke on the phone with medium Suzanne Northrop, who said she saw "three dogs" around my father's spirit. She said "one of them has short fur, almost like skin, and is very close to you, Rob." Suzanne went on to say, "In fact, this dog, very vivacious, like a puppy, has visited you and given you many signs." When I told her Buzz was a Weimaraner, the short fur made sense. Suzanne went on to tell me, "Buzz said you've held onto the responsibility for his passing and you need to let it go. He was only supposed to be with you a very short time."

There are many stories of ghost or spirit animals that can still be seen, heard or felt on Earth.

In his book, *Talking to Heaven*, James Van Praagh did a reading for a woman and he kept seeing her home from the view of being on the floor. He was also shown photos of dogs on her refrigerator, and finally he called out what turned out to be the woman's dog's name, who had passed two months before.

I heard further evidence during a seminar called "A Closer Look: After Death Communications" set up through *JaniceErvin.com* that Tom and I attended in Chantilly, Virginia on May 2, 2009. During the event, medium Barb Mallon was contacted by a beige "scruffy" Terrier and a black and white Cocker Spaniel, both of which had passed and belonged to a woman named Laura, who was attending the seminar. Laura sat there and listened to Barb describe the traits of her late Terrier named "Peanuts." Laura choked up with happiness knowing that her recently passed terrier was happy in the afterlife, and still watching out for her. The Cocker Spaniel had passed long before the Terrier, but they were together in the afterlife.

Following are some stories about my friend Craig's dog, Oprah, who passed as I was writing this book. Oprah gave Craig some sure signs that she was still around and watching over him.

OPRAH GIVES SIGNS SHE'S STILL WITH HER DAD

My friend Craig lives in Pasadena, Maryland, and had a beautiful Boxer her named "Oprah Winfrey" for the talk show hostess. Following is the story of how she came to be a big part of his life. Craig wrote this on his blog on Thursday, June 26, the day after Oprah passed away. Following Oprah's passing, Craig received two rather immediate and incredible signs that Oprah was still with him and watching out for him.

PHOTO: Oprah in 2008.
Credit: Craig B.

Craig wrote on June 26, 2008, "Oprah Winfrey born and originally named 'Sophie' on September 16, 1997, in the Groenwilde, Gauteng

Province of South Africa, died yesterday 10 weeks shy of her 11th Birthday."

"The first two years of her life she lived with me in Johannesburg, South Africa. She was an outside dog back then, but Daddy bought her an extra large Wendy-Hut Dog House and nice blankets from Makro, which made me feel guilty because I was buying better blankets for my dog than the local Zulu's slept with during the cold Transvaal Winters."

"She had a good life in South Africa; where a servant named Doris Seedpod fed her and talked to her all day while I was at work. Even though Doris spoke the language of Xhosa to Oprah, with what sounds like clicking. I think Oprah understood Doris, too. That's where I got the clicking sound that I used with her up until the very end to keep her calm. Even though I didn't know what the clicks meant, to me it was a signal that I was there and everything was alright."

"Oprah loved the Hoededa's, a bird the size of a turkey vulture which visited the gardens everyday - she'd chase them causing such a raucous of the famed call from the birds 'Ha-di-dah, Ha-di-dah, Ha-di-dah' which is how they came to be named."

"Then when things weren't working out for me in South Africa I left and had to leave Oprah behind with my roommate. But a telephone call came saying if I didn't return, the dog would be put down. So just after Easter, and just for the sole purpose of getting my dog, I returned to Johannesburg and took a leave of absence from my job in Washington. The ordeal took eight months, however, and I had to wait for the right time. That's why I called Oprah my 'Thirty Thousand Dollar Dog.'"

"That day came [when I was finally able to take Oprah home] and like an episode of the movie "Not without my Daughter" we fled. The servants packed all my belongings while I got the exportation paperwork completed and bought our tickets. I literally walked up to the counter and said I need a seat for myself, my dog and 400lbs of baggage ON THE FLIGHT THAT DAY. And KLM Royal Dutch Airlines accommodated us. I remember feeling safe once we were above the Belgian Congo and no longer in South African Airspace."

"KLM only lets animals fly one sector a day so Oprah was put up at the Schipol Airport Kennel overnight while I was flying home to Philadelphia. Then next day I went and picked up Oprah in Washington, D.C. at the airport. I can still see her in that crate on top of a forklift going BEEP BEEP BEEP. When she saw me it was like her heart emitted so much love, excitement and relief that Daddy was on the other side."

"Oprah became a very special and gentle dog here in America because she had so much exposure to other people every single day. Everyone loved that dog. I truly think giving her the name 'Oprah' helped. You can't help but smile at a boxer named Oprah."

"Oprah became everything to me: My companion, friend and child. She had the best life and was spoiled rotten with comfort and affection. She also had the best medical care at Anne Arundel Veterinary Hospital for many years. The staff there and at the Target Pharmacy knew me well because of 'a dog named Oprah.'"

"There are people who know my dog by name that I don't even know. When I would go on a walk, people young and old, would yell out 'OPRAH" and I'd be standing there wondering 'Who in the hell is that?' One time an old lady yelled out "You're beautiful" to which I responded "thank you" then paused and said "Oh, you meant the dog" and she howled laughing at my joke."

"Oprah started getting 'old' about 18 months before she passed, when she was diagnosed with Cushing's Disease. She was on Lysodren therapy until her last day to regulate the tumor growth on her adrenalin glands----Cushing's is something everyone should learn about---Does your dog suddenly look old? Is she drinking water constantly? Having trouble walking? Urinating a lot that it's noticeably significant?"

"Well, each sign of Cushing's can be dismissed as 'She's getting old, maybe its arthritis, panting a lot---maybe she's hot. Every symptom was something that could easily be dismissed. But having all of them at once is a problem and a dog should be checked. The Lysodren therapy eases all of them and in a few weeks the dog looks normal again. It works by producing more Cortisol and less adrenalin."

"During the last four days of her life, Oprah wasn't walking and was having trouble getting up. Then she refused to eat, refused to urinate, and was panting, so I made her an appointment. The next day her stomach was so bloated and distended I went into a panic. I took her to the animal hospital where they ran some tests. The doctor thought there were two things going on and possibly even Lyme disease."

"Her gums were grey and her eyes had a yellowy tint, in addition to the stomach bloating. He gave the dog a sedative, did some x-rays and then took a needle and inserted it in her abdomen. The fluid coming out was mostly blood and the x-rays confirmed cancer on the spleen, which had ruptured. He said that her blood tests came back indicating she was extremely anemic which was due to the internal bleeding."

"There was no guarantee that surgery at the specialty hospital would even work but it would cost $5,000 to start. She has a heart condition, is 11 years old, has Cushing's, past history of mast cell tumor removal last year and the doctor told me that basically right now she's bleeding to death and that in all honesty I should put her down."

"So yesterday I held my dog, my face to hers, made soft clicking noises and the shot was administered. She died peacefully and will now be cremated."

I wrote Craig back on his blog on June 26 and let him know that Oprah would, in fact, give him signs that she was still around and still watching out for him. It didn't take long.

Here's what I told him: Craig- It's so heart wrenching to lose your baby- you have our deepest sympathy.

I can relate to the hurt, because I went through it with little Buzz when he passed at 6 months. I truly feel your heartache, and I'm crying as I write this. But you must remember the love you shared.

Oprah was such a great girl, a true friend, and gave nothing but unconditional love. That's what our canine children do. It's what they're best at.

Your tribute to Oprah is incredible. The story is one of love. A love so deep you had for Oprah that you flew to South Africa to bring her home. I can't say I've ever heard of that much love and commitment before to a canine companion. That's what makes you such a great person.

The unconditional love that Oprah gave you returned your love for her.

As painful as it was to make the decision to let her go on to the next phase in her life, it was the most loving, unselfish thing you could do. She wanted to go home and play with other dogs in heaven. I'm saying a prayer and asking little Buzz to meet her there and play with her.

I want to let you know, though, that the love doesn't go away. Oprah will still be around, too. Her spirit, like Buzz's spirit, will let you know she's near you. Since Buzz passed, I've seen, felt and heard many signs from him. I'll explain more later, but keep an eye out. Oprah is devoted to her daddy and will be there to protect you all the time.

We'll call you later to check on you. I know it's difficult to talk now. This is an incredibly difficult time. We send our love and deepest sympathy to you.

Love, Rob and Tom

OPRAH GIVES VISIBLES SIGNS SHE'S AROUND

On June 25th, Craig noticed his first sign from Oprah and put it on his blog. "I cut the flowers tonight," he wrote. "These flowers bloomed the day Oprah died. The bush they grew on never ever bloomed until after 3:00 p.m. on June 25th. So I have them drying now. (His friend) Jim was with me. He said it was a message. Jim was right." This is just one sign that Oprah would be giving Craig that she was still around looking after her dad.

The next sign would come on July 4th and is probably one of the most incredibly touching signs I've ever heard about or seen.

PHOTO: Oprah's flower heart blooming in Craig's yard.
Credit: Craig B.

On Friday, July 4, Craig wrote and published on his blog, "This morning, that bush that never bloomed until Oprah died has now produced a HEART. I cut it and stuck it in a vase."

There is no such thing as a coincidence. These "coincidences" are spirits working around us to make things happen. Everything DOES happen for a reason.

OPRAH GIVES AN AUDITORY GREETING

I wrote to my friend Craig on July 8, 2008, to ask his permission to use his story about Oprah in this book. Although I expect that Oprah will continue to provide more signs to her dad that she's still around, I didn't expect the email I received so quickly with another.

Craig received Oprah's ashes, and spirits sometimes linger when their ashes are in a house. As long as there are people and emotions there to help provide energy for a spirit to manifest itself in sight, sound or other manners, spirits can send signs to the living.

Oprah's appearance this time was auditory, and she gave it to Craig's best friend, Jim, who basically shared Oprah with Craig for years. Following is Craig's email about Jim's experience in Craig's house. Jim was waiting for Craig to return from visiting his grandmother down the street, when Jim, who knew Oprah very well during her time on Earth, received a sign from her:

"Tue 7/08/08 9:32 PM

Rob! Jim was here in my house waiting for me 90 minutes, didn't realize I was down the street at my grandmother's house, and he heard her (Oprah's) toenails, claws.....anyway, he heard her clicking on the wood floor! - Craig"

CRAIG GETS A NEW DOG – GRACIE SENSES OPRAH'S SPIRIT

After Craig's dog Oprah passed, Craig wasn't thinking about getting another dog, but a grey Mastiff that one of his neighbors had adopted was too much for them to handle, so Craig adopted "Gracie."

In May 2009, Craig said that he would often sit at his kitchen table and eat dinner with his back facing the living room. Gracie would bark, growl or stare into the living room quite often.

When I visited Craig's house I knew immediately that Oprah's spirit was still there. I also asked Craig if Oprah used to sit under the window and look outside. He confirmed that. I told him that I felt that Oprah would come back every now and then and sit in her favorite spot, and that Gracie, like other dogs, can sense spirits. To Gracie, whenever Oprah's spirit would show up, it was like a living dog was in the house staring at her. That's why Gracie would stare at the window, because Oprah's bed used to be right underneath it. That's where Oprah used to love staying when she was alive. Remember, Earth-bound ghosts or spirits who have passed come back to the location they're most comfortable in or were last alive.

DIANE'S DOG TEGAN SENDS MESSAGES TO ME

Following are emails back and forth between our friend Diane (Di) and me in July 2009 when I was editing this book. During that month, Di's beloved cocker spaniel, Tegan, had to be euthanized because of a serious and sudden illness. Di was struggling over having to euthanize Tegan, and was agonizing over the suffering that Tegan experienced at the end her life. That is truly the hardest thing a pet owner can go through.

Tegan came to me with some messages that brought Diane peace and a happy, convincing surprise. This is an example of why I consider my ability a blessing to be used to help others.

PHOTO: Tegan.
Credit: Diane S.

Our emails:
From: DianeS
Date: Mon, 13 Jul 2009 08:28:27 -
0400
Subject: Tegan
To: rgutro

Thank you so much for ALL of
that...the problem is that Tegan wasn't sick..
Something happened to her brain and
basically, she went insane..mentally she was no longer "with us" as the
Vet at the Emergency Clinic told me..It was awful, Rob. I seem to be
always on the verge of tears..she was screaming and crying at the
end...I just don't know how to get past that.

In a message dated 7/13/2009 8:44:54 A.M. Eastern Daylight
Time, rgutro writes:

Di - It must have been something genetic. We knew a couple that
had a cavalier spaniel, and they suffer from a genetic disease where
their skulls are too small for their growing brains. I can't remember the
name of the disease, but it's genetic in some spaniels. They had to put
their dog down at 5 years old, as he was convulsing, whining, in
serious pain. There's nothing that can be done. What happens is the
brain grows backwards into the brain stem (toward the spine) as I
understand it, causing all kinds of pain and dysfunction.
You need to know that you did the best thing you could ever do for
Tegan. It was the most unselfish act of love and kindness, letting her
achieve peace and no pain. She's now with you. You know how I have
the ability to sense spirits. She's there beside you, and is so grateful for
your love. She's by your side. She says she loved being in the kitchen.
She knows how truly loved she was, and is so grateful for the short time
she was able to spend with you. All you have to do is call her and she'll
come by your side. She wants you to understand that it was a very
courageous thing that you did for her. She said that some moms
wouldn't have the courage, or wouldn't want to do what was best for
their dog, but you did. She said it was her time to go, and that she
wants you to focus on other dogs that may need your help, and she'll be
there to guide them along with you. She's going to follow along with

you in the car whenever you tend to other dogs. If you see a dog that you're tending stare at "empty space" or even growl at nothing, they're likely seeing Tegan.

She showed me some kind of red toy that she liked and wants you to hold onto it. I'm unsure if it's a rubber toy like a kong, or an animal, but she's showing me something red.

I hope this helps you. Tegan is telling me that the unconditional love you share will always be.

As you know, I've been through this, and it's never easy. The only comfort is the messages she can send to you - so watch for pennies on the ground, or strange things happening around the house. She'll be sending you little messages.

Tom and I are here for you, Diane.
Love, Rob

From: DianeS
Date: Tue, 14 Jul 2009 08:57:45 -0400
Subject: Re: Tegan
To: rgutro
Rob, You have no idea how much peace your email brought to me..I am reading it over and over again...I know you are right. They called yesterday to say that I could pick up her ashes. I am searching for the perfect memorial stone, but there are so many to choose from...
Love, Di

July 14, 2009
Di - I told Tom how Tegan came to me yesterday.

In fact, I'm getting a headache at the back of my head, which means there's a spirit here, and it's her again. She's licking my right leg. I'm unsure what that means. Maybe she's sending kisses to you- it's brought tears to my eyes! Wow. The love is really powerful. She says "Whichever stone you pick out will be the right one." She will steer you to the perfect one. She said she's happy and at peace and is showing me a wagging tail. She says "Thanks, Mom, I love you" and something about chicken or a chicken treat. I guess she liked them? That was it- she's not here anymore, but she'll be around you whenever you call her name. Wow.
Love, Rob

Re: Tegan
From: DianeS

Dogs can and do communicate with mediums, and Diane's dog coming to me reinforces that truth. Other mediums like Barb Mallon and James Van Praagh have also talked about their experiences with pets coming to them. Dogs, cats and horses will show the medium things that they identified with when they were among the living. They will also show a medium what they're focused on from their perspective. For example, a medium may look at something like a cabinet that holds dog treats looking up from the floor, where a dog would have been standing when it was alive.

The next part of this chapter focuses on a puppy I had that tragically passed in 2005. He turned out to be the world's best canine communicator.

MY PUPPY BUZZ – THE WORLD'S BEST CANINE COMMUNICATOR

The year before I met Tom, I was living in a home in Odenton and had a roommate, Jay. He had an older Border Collie named Solo. On October 17, 2004, Jay surprised me with a 3-month-old Weimaraner puppy for my birthday that I named "Buzz Wyatt." Buzz was born on July 29, 2004.

I honestly didn't think I was ready to raise a dog, but I immediately fell in love with this beautiful grey pup with the beautiful green eyes. In the short time that we enjoyed together, Buzz was with me every minute.

PHOTO: Buzz Wyatt listening on Oct. 30, 2004.
Credit: R.Gutro

The week after "adopting" Buzz, named for my nickname for drinking too much coffee, the kennel cough that he came to me with became serious. It turned into pneumonia. Not knowing what to do, I took him to the 24-hour emergency room in Annapolis, Maryland (they offer excellent care). Pneumonia was confirmed, and Buzz had to stay for a couple of nights. He received heavy antibiotics, and was on oxygen. I was a mess.

When Buzz came home, I nursed him back to health over a couple of weeks. I spent several days and nights having him breathe in steam from a vaporizer, with a towel over his little head. He didn't know what was going on, but I remember how patient he was. Buzz slept in my bed with me and never left my side. He became my best friend and we really bonded.

My roommate had severe anger issues and often scared Buzz and me. It was a tough situation. I would often take Buzz places to be away from the house until the house could be sold. Foolishly, I bought into the house with him as an investment while renting my own townhouse elsewhere. That was a lesson learned. Not being able to pay two mortgages, I couldn't move until the Odenton house was sold, which happened in summer 2005, but I'm getting ahead of myself.

I would walk Buzz and my roommate's dog in the neighborhood morning and night. The dogs became my responsibility. It was challenging at times, but Buzz showed me what unconditional love was for the first time in my adult life.

THE ACCIDENT – BUZZ PASSES AWAY

Tuesday night, February 22, 2005, I had to say good-bye to one of the best friends I've ever had. That night, I was walking the dogs, 6-month old Buzz and 6-year old Solo, as usual around 5 p.m., and Buzz was exceptionally excited. While walking on Strawberry Lake Way in Odenton, Buzz saw an old man and his dog across the street, and Buzz wanted to run to him.

While he was pulling hard, I grabbed the leash near the end, and the clasp opened! Before I knew what happened, Buzz ran into the street. In an instant, a car driving about 50 mph in the 30-mph zone struck and killed him as he stepped off the curb and out of my reach, just feet away from where I was standing in shock.

I knelt beside him and felt the warmth leave his precious little body. I never saw the car, and the driver never came over to me to check on the condition of my puppy. I'm unsure if the driver was in shock herself, or simply didn't care. I only know that the woman who killed Buzz never came over to offer her apologies or sympathies. Looking back on the situation, it's difficult to believe that some people can be so heartless. Regardless, I was in no condition to even think about it at the time.

The next thing I knew, four or five neighbors from Strawberry Lake Way rushed to my aid. Sandra Sartwell, a woman who would later become a good friend, delivered *The Capital* newspaper and the *West County News*, and was driving by and immediately pulled her car over and jumped to my side. She sat with me and called my roommate Jay and the police. She made sure that I was not alone. I have never forgotten the love she showed me that day. I know that she was sent to me at that time to comfort me.

Another kind woman held Jay's dog, Solo. Unfortunately, I can't recall her name. From across the street, another neighbor, Ed Brown, and his son brought blankets and towels and wrapped Buzz's body. Cathy Spry, who was driving a pickup truck, pulled over. She and several other neighbors put Buzz's lifeless body in the back of her truck and she drove him to my home. I will never forget these incredible people as long as I live.

Once home, we lifted Buzz's body into the back of my pick-up truck and went inside to figure out what to do next.

I wrote an article of thanks to the neighbors that appeared in the *Annapolis Capital* newspaper on March 13, 2005. It was called "Good deeds: Readers give thanks - Neighbors come to aid after puppy killed." The article appeared here, although the link may now be disabled: *http://www.hometownannapolis.com/cgi-bin/read/2005/03_13-71/TOP*

I later met many others at a grief group for dog owners, and several of them had read the story in the newspaper and knew who I was.

THE FIRST SIGN FROM BUZZ

When my roommate and I first walked in the house after putting Buzz's little body in the back of my pick-up truck, Alan Jackson's song "My heart is empty like a Monday morning church" was playing on the radio. It's a song about a man whose loved one passed away. It was too much of a coincidence, and there is NO such thing as a coincidence, as I mentioned before in this book.

I called the vet and told them Buzz was killed by a car. I told them that I wanted his ashes. They told me to bring his body over as soon as I could. My roommate and I waited for my friend Terry to arrive from about 30 miles away. She drove to the house immediately to transport little Buzz to the vet hospital with us. She, my roommate and I arrived around 7 p.m. and met Jay's friend Jackie there. When we arrived, the nurses came and took Buzz's little body to prepare him for us to say goodbye. Then we experienced the next sign he was still around.

THE SECOND SIGN: MOVING AN OBJECT

We waited outside of the vet hospital, in the parking lot beside the building, for a good five minutes. In the back of the building, about 30 feet from where we were all standing, suddenly, a lid popped off a trash can and came crashing on the ground. We looked over and there was no one, human or animal around, and there was no wind. We knew that it had to be a sign from Buzz to let us know that he's still here. Once we got inside the hospital, we stood around his little body, holding him, praying for him, and said goodbye to him. It was devastating as you can imagine.

PHOTO: Buzz napping.
Credit: R.Gutro

THE THIRD SIGN FROM BUZZ: MUSICAL

After saying goodbye to Buzz, Jay and I returned to the house. When we opened the door, the radio was still playing. What was extremely unnerving was that it was playing Garth Brooks' 1990 song called "The Dance." The song's lyrics say "I could have missed the pain, but I would never miss the Dance." It's about the pain of losing someone that you deeply love, but despite the pain, you wouldn't give up the time you had with them. Again, it was a message, and simply too odd to be a coincidence.

STRANGE REACTIONS IN THE OTHER DOG

It's been said that dogs can sense and see spirits and ghosts when people can't. It's true. If you see a dog simply staring at what you think is an empty space, it's likely that the dog sees a human or animal spirit there. That spirit may even be talking to the dog.

My roommate's dog, Solo, had witnessed the entire accident, as I was walking him and Buzz together. Solo was on the other side of me at the time, and suddenly stopped and he sat on the sidewalk when Buzz was struck and killed in front of us. He eventually walked over and sniffed Buzz, so I knew he was aware of what happened.

The February night that Buzz died, Solo began acting strangely. Since Buzz's arrival into the house the previous October, Solo had stopped playing with toys. However, when Jay and I brought him back to the house immediately after the accident, he picked up Buzz's toy monkey and badger and played with them. Today, those two toys sit next to the wooden box containing Buzz's ashes in my house.

The day after Buzz's accident, Solo was whining to go out on the back deck that Buzz used to love. We didn't understand, as Solo never whined or wanted to go there. We thought it had to be little Buzz calling him out there. It happened several times.

THE MOST HELPFUL EMAIL FROM A CLOSE FRIEND

I have never forgotten the email my good friend Lynn J. wrote to me after Buzz died. Lynn saw me break down at work and cry over Buzz often. During the first week I was a total mess. Lynn's email really helped, and I printed it, and read it over and over every night. I'm reprinting it here with permission, in the hope that it will also comfort anyone who has lost a dog or a cat or other pet who had become a best friend.

From: Lynn J.
To: Rob G.
Date: February 2005
Rob, I was the same way when (my dog) Jeff died. I couldn't function AT ALL for about a week afterwards, then little by little (over some months), the pain subsided and I was left with many, many happy memories of a wonderful companion. I did have Jeff for eight wonderful years, but even then, I felt his life was cut short. He was diagnosed with brain cancer, and within four days after the diagnosis he was gone. My advice, for what it's worth is to stay busy, smile at the good times, keep pictures around (as you have done) not to keep you sad, but to help you remember that you are better off having had Buzz in your life, if only for seven months. I always like to think that when I die, all my pets will be there waiting for me, tails wagging, practically leaping out of their skin to get to me and lick me. I will throw my arms around them, feel their soft fur again, bury my head in their necks to smell that wonderful warm, doggy smell, feel their heartbeat right next to mine, and then I will know that I've reached heaven. Take care of yourself and know that I am thinking of you.

Lynn

THE NEXT STEP IN THE STORY – A NEW PUPPY

Our friends can play amazing roles in our lives. Each person that comes into our life is there for a very good reason. Some teach us tough lessons, like breaking our hearts. Some are like guardian angels who offer support like Sandra who stayed with me when Buzz was killed; or Lynn J. who wrote that email. Another friend was responsible for bringing back love into my life, by convincing me to rescue another dog in Buzz's memory.

After a week, my friend and co-worker, Lynn C. went on Weimaraner rescue Web Sites and looked for desperate puppies needing a home. She printed out a number of them and brought them to me. She said it would be a nice tribute to Buzz. She was 100 percent right.

So, on March 11, 2005, I decided to get another puppy of the same breed as Buzz – a Weimaraner. I found a three month old pup named "Chloe," whom I would later name Dolly Loretta, on a Web Site for the Wolf Creek Weimaraner Rescue in Knoxville, Tennessee. I spoke with Amber of the Rescue over the phone to learn about Chloe's (hereafter called "Dolly") history. Dolly was one of six puppies in a litter in Atlanta, Georgia, born Nov. 29th, 2004. Her mother contracted tetanus, and couldn't feed the pups, so the owners called a shelter. The Atlanta shelter couldn't handle the pups and called Wolf Creek. Amber and one of her colleagues drove to Atlanta and brought them back to Knoxville. She said they had to bottle feed all six pups for two months.

On March 12 my friend Jeff and I made the 9 ½ hour drive (each way) and met Dolly at the shelter. We played with her for about an hour and then bought all new dog stuff at a local Petsmart. We stayed at a hotel overnight, picked Dolly up the next morning and drove back to Maryland. She was the perfect pup.

Buzz wanted to let me know that adopting Dolly Loretta was a great thing, and he wanted to show me he approved. The first way he did that was to let me know he was around through temperature changes.

FOURTH SIGN: TEMPERATURE CHANGES

As described previously, spirits manifest themselves by drawing the energy out of the air and create "cold spots." My father did that the night he died when he came to me and hugged me. Buzz did it, too.

On May 23, 2005, a warm spring day, I awoke at 5:30 a.m. and let Dolly and my roommate's dog, Solo, out into the backyard. I brought them into the kitchen to feed them. I placed their bowls on the kitchen counter and went to mix some wet food into Dolly's bowl with her dry food. Suddenly, the entire left side of my body, from the middle of my forehead all the way down, became icy cold, while the right side of me was warm and even perspiring from the warmth in the house. I sensed Buzz Wyatt's presence, turned to my left, looked toward the floor and called his name out loud. The cold feeling on my left side faded quickly.

Dolly was still sitting to my right, and Solo was sitting behind her, unmoving. I had experienced cold spots before, and I know it was Buzz letting me know that he was still there waiting for his breakfast. Dogs like to stick to schedules, and Buzz was doing that even after he passed!

FIFTH SIGN: PREMONITION OR MESSAGE?

One of the strangest experiences I've ever had was a premonition of danger, in a message sent from my puppy Buzz.

Wednesday, June 22, 2005, marked four months to the day that Buzz was killed. Oddly enough, that day marked the same exact age Buzz was and that my new puppy Dolly was. Buzz was born on July 29, 2004, and died on February 22, 2005. He was 6 months and 23 days old, and the accident occurred around 5 p.m. eastern time. Dolly was born on November 29, exactly four months later than Buzz. On June 22, 2005, she was also 6 months and 23 days old.

Over the first two weeks of June, I had a feeling of dread about June 22nd. I couldn't explain it. I mentioned it to my roommate the week before, while we were walking our two dogs. As the day loomed closer, my feelings of dread continued. I now know that it was Buzz sending me a message this was the day he had died, and he wanted to make sure Dolly was safe.

I arrived home around 5:30 p.m. eastern daylight savings time (EDT), which is 4:30 p.m. (ET) eastern standard time. I mention the time, because of the time Buzz was killed when his leash opened.

Jay departed for school by 5:55 p.m. EDT, and I leashed up both dogs. I made sure that I put our blue leash on Dolly, as it had a safety clasp on it. Solo, who was 7 years old at the time, was very obedient and also leashed, but I don't have to worry about him running away. I decided to walk the dogs to the mailbox this time, instead of going out and around the neighborhood, where I sometimes take them. A short time later, I would find out why Buzz steered me away from where he was killed.

Those four months ago with Buzz, I had taken him on the main street, called Strawberry Lake Way. It was then that he saw a dog on the other side of the street and he pulled on the leash as I was holding it near the clasp, and it opened. Immediately as he stepped off the sidewalk, an inattentive driver, speeding too close to the curb, hit him and broke his neck, killing him instantly.

Back to June 22, 2005. I walked Dolly and Solo to the mailbox located within the townhouse complex and got the mail. We walked a little way into the woods. The dogs were pulling unusually strong, and I got a deep feeling of dread. I said out loud, "No. This is just what happened with Buzz. He was pulling excessively and unusually that day, just before the accident happened." So, we turned to go back home. As we neared the mailboxes again (we were about 15 to 20 feet from the street), suddenly, the blue safety leash on Dolly had come off! Thankfully, because of Buzz's messages, I was watching Dolly closely when it happened.

I couldn't understand how the leash could come undone after about 15 minutes of walking. I immediately grabbed her collar and refastened the leash to it. I noticed that it was around the same time in the evening, 5:05 p.m. ET or 6:05 p.m. EDT, when Buzz was killed and a similar thing had happened. This was too strange and unnerving to be coincidence. Buzz had warned me in advance.

I took Solo and Dolly home immediately. I was light-headed. I was shaking, but I had a sense of relief. The dreaded time had passed, and Dolly was okay. She will be okay from now on, I thought. It was a little later that I realized that Buzz was telling me that this was a way to say, "You've saved Dolly, and now you can forgive yourself for what happened to me." I had run the scenario of his accident over and over in my head in the last four months asking myself what I could have done to prevent it.

SIXTH SIGN: ANOTHER MUSICAL MESSAGE

Another sign from Buzz came when Jay got home, which oddly, was around 8 p.m., the same time that we returned from the animal hospital four months to the day before, after saying goodbye to Buzz for the last time. I had the radio playing, just as it was that February 22. Jay asked me to help him with a school project right after he got home. As we started working on his homework the exact same old country song, "The Dance" by Garth Brooks, played on the radio, just as it had when we walked into house after saying goodbye to Buzz at the animal hospital in February 2005. As I write this, I have chills. Jay acknowledged it as it played in the background. Was that a coincidence? No. It was Buzz sending a message that he's still around, and was still watching out for me.

SEVENTH SIGN: MUSICAL SIGN AND A MOVED OBJECT

On Saturday, June 25, 2005, in a fit of anger, Jay knocked over the wooden box containing Buzz's ashes and the pictures of Buzz that surrounded it from a pedestal in the house. He felt badly about it. I was horrified. On the following Wednesday evening, Jay was listening to a CD in his car coming home from work, and when he took it out, Garth Brooks' "The Dance" was playing on the radio. Perhaps Buzz was telling Jay he was forgiven for knocking over his ashes.

Just as Buzz caused the trash can lid to fly off at the vet hospital the night he died, he moved a household object, too. After Jay was home for a short time on June 25th, he started walking to the front door, where Buzz always used to get excited and pick up shoes. Jay stopped and watched as one of two shoes moved sideways and nothing was there to move it. We both believe Buzz wanted to let Jay know that he's still playing in the house. In the months that followed, the house was sold, and Dolly and I moved into another house by ourselves.

PHOTO: Buzz's ashes in the wooden box, with his favorite badger and gorilla stuffed toys next to it.
Credit: R.Gutro

EIGHTH SIGN: "BUZZ" MAKES AN APPEARANCE TO A FRIEND IN ANOTHER STATE: 2006

Spirits of dogs, like people, are not limited to geographic areas in bringing signs. That's how a medium located anywhere in the world can get readings from people who lived and died in other parts of the world.

It's also possible that someone who may not have even met the person or pet can get a sign, if they know enough about them. That's what happened to a friend of mine who lives in New Hampshire.

My friend Lisa who lives in Portsmouth, New Hampshire relayed this story to me on November 2, 2006: "I thought of you and Dolly and especially Buzz last week when I was out running in Portsmouth. Picture the scene, a paved road through the forest on a cloudless, crisp, fall day - all quiet except the birds singing at 7:30 a.m. I round a corner and a beautiful version of Dolly/Buzz comes running out of the woods and runs up to me, tail wagging, then promptly sits in the road directly in front of me. I had to make a choice - run around the dog or stop and say "hello." I chose the latter and before I knew it I was getting a doggy hug and kisses from this sweet dog. The dog was wearing a tag and you'll never guess what his name was?! "Buzzy." And...he was owned by Rob Gatzby - How's that for a coincidence?! I think Buzz whispered in Buzzy's ear to say "hi." After our encounter, he disappeared in the woods and I've never seen him again. Truth is stranger than fiction."

NINTH SIGN: BUZZ MAKES HIS FIRST VISIBLE AND AUDIBLE APPEARANCE

I don't often see spirits visibly, but this was the fourth time I've actually seen one as clearly as I see a living person or animal.

In late November, 2007 I was cleaning up the kitchen in my townhouse around 9:30 p.m. I lived only with my dog Dolly, and was readying to move into a house with my partner Tom. But that night, only my dog Dolly and I were in the old townhouse, and Tom and his dog were at their house.

The galley kitchen in that townhouse sat between the dining room and living room, and from it I could see into the dining room. Parallel to the kitchen is a small hallway that also connects the two rooms.

As I was cleaning the counter, I heard the sound of a dog's nails walking on the hardwood floor, and then heard a collar jingle. I thought nothing of it because Dolly was in the house somewhere. I poked my head around the corner and peered into the dining room to see the back of a Weimaraner disappear as it walked down the hallway toward the living room. Of course, I thought it was Dolly.

I called Dolly by name, and there was no response. I figured that Dolly jumped on the living room couch, where she sometimes liked to lay down, and she curled up to sleep.

I followed the dog into the living room and looked on the couch. There was no dog there and I didn't hear another sound. The dog couldn't have passed me and gone into another room.

I turned around and went upstairs. When I got to my bedroom, I saw Dolly there, curled up on my bed and sound asleep. She had no collar on. When I came back downstairs, I saw her collar hanging up on the coat hook. I knew then it was Buzz's spirit letting me know that he was still in the house with Dolly and me, and was just checking in.

TENTH SIGN: MORE MUSICAL SIGNS

On February 22, 2007, two years to the day after Buzz was killed, I bought a dozen red roses at lunchtime. After work, I picked up my dog Dolly and drove to the spot on Strawberry Lake Way where Buzz was killed. As I have on that same day every year since he passed, I dropped one red rose on the sidewalk on that spot.

I said a prayer and got back in the truck. I had been listening to Tammy Wynette's Greatest Hits CD, and decided to punch the radio button. That's when I heard one of the three songs that were playing that fateful day Garth Brooks' song, "The Dance," the very same song that was playing in the Odenton house right after the accident. Of course, it brought tears to my eyes, but it was Buzz's way of letting me know that he acknowledged the rose.

This is no coincidence because "The Dance" is a 17-year-old song, not aired much. What's even more odd was that it just "happened" to start (it was on the first 10 notes) when I switched from listening to a CD to listening to the radio.

Buzz also gave me a musical sign first thing that morning, too. When I awoke and put the radio on, one of the other songs that reminded me of him, "One More Day" by Diamond Rio was playing on the radio. That song was six years old and also not played much. It was a reminder from Buzz of what day it was. It was an emotional day for me.

ELEVENTH SIGN: BUZZ GIVES A SIGN AROUND WATER

Moving water provides energy that enables spirits or Earth-bound ghosts to communicate. The spirit of a friend's mother came to me when I was in the shower, and Buzz provided a sign around water, too.

In February 2007, I read John Grogan's great book, *Marley and Me* (now a hit movie on DVD). It's a heartwarming and true story about how the author and his wife adopted a yellow Labrador Retriever puppy they named "Marley" and had adventures. Marley "grew into a barreling, 97-pound steamroller of a Labrador Retriever, a dog like no other." The book takes you through their entire life with Marley, and, ends at the dog's death from old age.

I was reading the last chapter of the book before I was planning to take a shower and turn in for the evening. I just finished the book and was sobbing over the ending, when I said aloud, "Buzz." It immediately made me think of the pain of losing my six month old puppy. I got myself together, went into the bathroom and took a nice warm shower hoping to clear my head. I was still thinking of Buzz.

I turned the water off and pulled the shower curtain back. As I was about to step out of the shower and get my towel, I watched it slide off the hook that it had been on for the last 12 hours, almost as if it were being pulled down to the ground by a dog, holding it by his teeth. I knew it was Buzz. He gave me a sign to let me know that he is still with me.

TWELFTH SIGN: BUZZ'S SECOND VISIBLE APPEARANCE

Back in the chapter on my father's passing I mentioned that I saw my dad walk into the light in August 2008. This is the last time I actually physically saw Buzz, too. When my Dad was walking toward the light at the cemetery (after the services), Buzz was sitting in the light, next to the two dogs my family had, Penny a beige cocker spaniel, and Gigi, a white poodle. All three dogs were sitting on the side of the light next to other family members as I watched my Dad walk into it and the light faded. It was good to see him one more time.

THE ART OF REIKI - COMMUNICATING WITH ANIMALS ALIVE OR PASSED

When Buzz was killed, I was totally distraught and an emotional mess. When your emotions are so overcome with grief, it's next to impossible to focus and meditate to enable communication with a spirit.

A couple of weeks after Buzz passed, my friend Terry suggested that I contact her friend Fay to communicate with Buzz for me. Fay worked in the art of Reiki. I had never heard of Reiki before, but learned that Reiki is basically a mediation that enables one to tune into information that is around all of us, such as spiritual or emotional energy.

According to Reiki.org, "Reiki is a Japanese technique for stress reduction and relaxation that also promotes healing. It is administered by "laying on hands" and is based on the idea that an unseen "life force energy" flows through us and is what causes us to be alive." Reiki taps into energy and spirits and ghosts are made of energy, thus, the meditation provides the ability to connect with them.

Reiki acknowledges that if someone's life energy is low, then they're more likely to develop sickness, be stressed or depressed. However, if the life energy is high, that's an indication of health and happiness.

The actual word "Reiki" comes from two Japanese words. The first, Rei means "God's Wisdom or the Higher Power" and Ki which is "life force energy." Put them together and Reiki is "spiritually guided life force energy."

Terry sent me an email about Reiki and explained it this way: *"Some people call it an "intuition." If you look into the whole Reiki experience, you will find that it's really an extension of holistic healing that has been around for hundreds of years. Go to http://www.reiki.org/ to get info to calm your nerves. It has everything to do with having an open mind and accepting the nonverbal communication that animals give us. The only thing that has to do with God, is that they do acknowledge that the information comes from a higher power."*

BUZZ COMMUNICATES THROUGH REIKI

One night in early March, 2005, about two weeks after Buzz's passing, I went to Terry's house. Terry called Fay for me and let me talk with her. Fay had never met me in person and only talked to me via email. She knew that Buzz was a Weimaraner, and knew his date of birth. I also told her how he passed, but nothing else.

Fay meditated as I waited on the phone for a couple of minutes. She asked about a certain toy that Buzz had and named it. I was surprised. Terry didn't even know about that specific toy (it was a black gorilla that squeaked, and that Buzz had chewed the nose off). That same toy is sitting next to his photo and his ashes in our house now.

Fay said that Buzz had crossed over and was happily playing in a field "like he was chasing butterflies." The next thing Fay said really threw me for a loop. She said, "Buzz tells me that you had a goofy nickname for your (former) roommate. One that you two only said to each other (It was "Trollie" as in "troll"). There was no way that she could know that, either, unless she was talking with Buzz or my roommate's dog Solo. This was the first time that I realized that dogs on the other side can, in fact, tell people things in a way in which mediums can translate to words.

Fay continued to tell me that Buzz said he was okay and that it was his time. She said that he was meant only to be on Earth a short time, but in that time, he taught me about unconditional love (he certainly did). Fay went on to say that Buzz was an "old soul," and you can get that feeling looking at a photo of his green eyes. He said he was here for the short mission of teaching me about love, and his time was over. Further, it was now my time to show that unconditional love to my new pup Dolly, who I adopted from Wolf Creek Weimaraner Rescue.

I hung up the phone with tears in my eyes, but having a much better understanding of why Buzz was only in my life for a very short time and that he was really at peace. I also knew that I needed to focus my love and energies on my new pup, Dolly, so I did.

A REIKI SESSION AMONG GRIEVING PET OWNERS WORKS

Fay, who works in Maryland, contacted me a month later in March 2005 to check on me. I had just attended a pet grief session for people who lost their dogs and cats, and met a number of people there. All of those at the session were all grieving and needed comfort, so I asked Fay if she would be interested in hosting a group of people in my home to cope with their losses, including me. She said yes. Following is Fay's email, to provide an idea about how she set up the group (reprinted here with her permission).

From: REIKISPEAK@aol.com
Date: Mon, 28 Mar 2005 09:28:06 EST

Hi Rob,
I'm glad to hear that Dolly is working out. I'm sure you will feel Buzz around as she learns the ropes! He seemed to really want her to be a part of your lives.

I got your message to learn more about some of the kinds of seminars I do.

What I would suggest doing, would be to set up something for several hours (up to 4) where everyone comes together. We can talk about general issues and give a brief back ground description if you like and then we can talk to the individual animals one at a time. We can do it in a group situation unless someone is uncomfortable doing it that way. It seems to really help people come to terms with their losses when they can share with others. After I have communicated with all the animals, I can walk everyone through some guided meditation/relaxation techniques and then everyone will have a change to "speak" with an animal.

I guide you through the whole process, and people are always amazed that they can do it. Truly, everyone is capable of communicating in the way that I do, they just don't trust their instincts. Depending on how interested people are, we can go a step further and each of you can communicate with one of the animals who has passed (not their own pet as that is too difficult when you begin). I recommend that people bring pictures of their pets as it helps them to visualize the process a little easier.

Twelve people is the maximum number of people per seminar. If you have less, that's okay. I do these to help the people and pets and generating income is a secondary issue for me. The other way that it can be done is to have people come for appointments at 1/2 hour intervals. These would be private sessions.

If either of these ideas appeals to you, let me know and we can set it up. If you have a different idea, please feel free to tell me about it as I am open to helping in any way I can.

Give my best to Dolly. I was so happy to be able to help you deal with the loss of Buzz. It truly was my pleasure!
Hugs back to you!
Fay

In April 2005, I organized a group of people who were still grieving from the loss of their pets, to meet at my townhouse. Fay came to the house and introduced Reiki. She taught everyone some meditations and handed out photos of dogs, cats and birds that had passed. She asked everyone to try and tune it to the animal by looking at the animal's eyes in the photos.

After looking at the photos and meditating, several of us, myself included, told what we were feeling about the environment, habits and personalities of the animals in the photo we were given. I had a photo of a bird that I was able to provide details on that weren't apparent from the photo. I amazed myself. Fay confirmed the details on the personalities, locations and habits for each animal. Some were able to tune in, such as myself, my roommate at the time, and a few others, while others couldn't focus. That proved to me that meditation really helped when communicating with spirits.

Fay can still be reached at *REIKISPEAK@aol.com* for anyone interested in the art of Reiki, or anyone who wants to communicate with a beloved pet that may have passed.

DOGS CAN ALSO SEE SPIRITS

Just as people can see and feel spirits, dogs can see them, too. Dogs can also hear spirits. People, however, have to use a digital audio recorder because they can't hear at the range a dog can hear.

On May 5, 2009, at 6 a.m. EDT, our friend Craig wrote on his Facebook page, "The dog (Gracie) is barking at the living room again! Crazy barking too. See it's that damned TV show I watched about a spooked house." Although Craig was jesting about the dog barking because he had watched a show on ghosts the night before, he knew it was because there was a spirit in his house.

A response came from Angie G.H. at 6:49 a.m. on May 5, 2009 that said "You know what that means? You have visitors. Check out my website: *www.easternshoreghosts.com.*"

Here are some examples that show that dogs see ghosts and spirits. One is when a dog reacts as he/she would when an actual person walks into the room, but there's no one there. It's easy to test that theory if you live in a haunted house, or bring your dog to a building that is known to have a presence.

One instance I can cite is the first time our Dachshund Franklin was taken to my partner's grandmother's grave. The dog had never been there. However, when he got out of the car, he ran directly to Tom's grandmother's grave and sat on it. He obviously saw her there.

Dogs have heightened senses. They may not have better vision than humans, but they are able to sense movement and hear at a higher pitch. Spirits are energies, and if you've ever heard of electronic voice phenomena (EVP), you'll know that spirits can make noises at pitches humans can't hear. Chapter 18 contains actual stories that provide evidence.

So, watch your dog closely, and pay attention to odd behavior. If they act like there is another person in the room, most likely there is someone there but they're just not alive.

OUR DOGS DOLLY AND FRANKLIN ACKNOWLEDGE BEVERLEE'S SPIRIT

Our Friend Beverlee A. of Baltimore passed away on March 29, 2009, at 5 p.m. EDT at the Future Care Nursing Home. Beverlee was 86 years old, and would have been 87 on May 21st. I met Beverlee in 2005 through our friend Terry. Bev was a sharp woman, with a great sense of humor who enjoyed living in the present and was extremely street-savvy.

We'd talk about politics, ghosts, religion, people, family, dogs, her past, home renovations, the weather, and anything else. Bev had been in the Navy, and often told me about her husband, Howard, who passed when they were in their 40s. She loved Howard with all her heart, and now she's together with him.

Bev mentioned to me that when she was a young girl, her mother passed away. Bev said that her mother's spirit visited her one night when she was in her bedroom. Bev firmly believed in ghosts and spirits.

When Bev was alive, I would visit her about every 2 weeks or so with Dolly (our Weimaraner) and sometimes Franklin (our Dachshund). I always bought Dunkin' Donuts coffee and her favorite vanilla cream-filled donut. She loved them, so I'd always bring a half-dozen and watch her eyes light up.

She was so excited when Tom and I found each other, and she said "he's the one you'll spend the rest of your life with." Of course, she was right. I will always cherish my visits with Bev. She loved seeing Tom and I, Dolly and Franklin. I loved talking with her about everything. I know that she's now at peace and reunited with her husband Howard after waiting some 45 years. The week she passed, I had Dunkin' Donuts coffee and vanilla cream donuts in her honor.

It was about two months after Beverlee's passing that her niece organized a memorial service for Beverlee. It was held at the retirement apartment building where she lived for many years, because there were many friends she left behind there. The service was held in the "penthouse" level, which was used for functions. It was set up with a little podium, seats and a piano. The minister from Beverlee's church led the service, and one of the congregation members played some hymns on the piano while everyone sang a few songs during the short ceremony.

As soon as we got upstairs to the level where the service was being held, little Franklin the Dachshund started shivering and whining. It was as if he noticed Beverlee's late cat, "Stitch," in the room. Franklin didn't stop whining the entire time, and he's never done that before. When we left, Franklin stopped.

PHOTO: Our dogs, Dolly the Weimaraner and Franklin the Dachshund, April 2008.
Credit: R.Gutro

Dolly gave a more noticeable sign. The minister had started the ceremony and said, "Let us pray." There was seconds of silence until Dolly let out one very loud and short bark! Dolly was acknowledging that Beverlee was there in the room, and apparently she was with her cat that had passed, at least according to Franklin!

CHAPTER 18
Ghost/Spirit Stories From Others: Part One

This chapter is devoted to encounters that friends, colleagues or acquaintances have had with spirits or strange phenomena. The chapter begins with stories from a mother and son of their encounters. This reinforces my belief that this ability is genetic. The stories that follow are in alphabetical order by U.S. state. After each story, I offer comments as "Editor's Notes" to provide insight into what was likely happening.

A MOTHER AND SON'S EXPERIENCES IN KANSAS AND CALIFORNIA

In Chapter 8: My Life Among Ghosts and Spirits, I mentioned that I believe that the ability to communicate with ghosts and spirits may be inherited. It is in my family, as my grandfather on my mother's side, my mother, and I have had communications with ghosts or spirits. The first collection of stories are from Betty and Richard Bent. They are mother and son.

Betty Bent was born March 2, 1922 in Hutchinson, Kansas and grew up there. Her father was a plumber, and her mother worked in the home. Betty shared her stories with her son Richard, who transcribed them. Richard has also had some experiences, which are printed after his mother Betty's events. Betty shared six encounters, all of which follow in date order of occurrence.

BETTY'S STORY #1: 1941 – PSYCHIC FEELINGS

Betty Bent told the following story: "When I was in junior college in 1941, in Hutchinson, Kansas, my art teacher, Barbara Bush (no relation to the former U.S. President's mother) invited me to go with her and two other teachers on a drive to Lindsborg, Kansas, to meet the famous Swedish artist, Birger Sandzin, and take a tour of his studio."

"When the teachers introduced themselves to the artist, I was tongue-tied to be in the presence of this great and gentle man. He smiled at me and took my hand in both of his and invited us to make ourselves at home and wander through his studio. It was a huge two-story building back of his home. The grey railing on the balcony was decorated with Indian blankets. His daughter, Margaret, came to meet us and she was jolly and talkative, just the opposite personality of her father."

"One Saturday 20 years later, at 10:25 in the morning, while at home and living in Compton, California, a suburb of Los Angeles, the thought flashed in my mind: "Birger Sandzen had died." The next day while reading the *Los Angeles Times newspaper,* I saw an article that said that the Swedish artist had died on Saturday at 10:25 a.m. I don't know why this happened, but I became much more interested in spirit communication and discussed it with a friend who believed in such things."

EDITOR'S COMMENT: In the spirit world, all things are connected. Psychics allow themselves to have a deeper connection to the environment around them, because they don't let the logical side of their brain always rule. They are open –minded. This accounts for their ability to sense things such people passing. In 2007, I met a young woman named Sarah who has the frightening ability to dream about people before they pass. She must have a strong connection to the spirit world to get these messages.

BETTY'S STORY #2: 1943 – A HELPFUL ASSIST FROM BEYOND?

Betty Bent told the following story: "During World War II, my father decided that the best way to help out the war effort was to accept a position in Portland, Oregon, as a steam fitter on the Liberty Ships. My dad was very excited about this opportunity, as he had never seen a ship or the ocean."

"I was 21 years old and it was our second day in Portland and I went out to find a job. My office experience had been in the insurance department of an investment company. I looked up an investment company in the phone book and made plans to take the bus into town. Once off the bus I realized that I had no clue as to where anything was and felt lost and disheartened."

"Almost immediately, a young Mexican looking man appeared by my side. He said, "This is the bus you want," pointing to a bus as it made its way towards us. He said, "I will go with you." I had not told him yet where I was going but he knew. He also asked me to speak Spanish so I would relax and feel more at ease with him. I had taken two years of Spanish in school but he wouldn't have known this. Soon, he had us off the bus and he took me to the building where I needed to go."

"I went in to speak to a nice gentleman in the insurance department of the investment company. He said he didn't have anything at the moment but his good friend who was Captain of the

Portland Port of Embarkation, needed office help. He gave me directions on how to get there. I came out of the building and my new friend was waiting for me."

"Before I could tell him where I was headed, he said, "This is the bus we take and I will go with you." We arrived at the gates to the Port of Embarkation. I was admitted and taken to a building where I was interviewed and my office skills were tested. I passed the tests, was signed up for a Civil Service job and was escorted out. I was told to report to work in three days."

"When I was escorted back to the gates, my new friend was still there waiting for me. He put me on a bus and said, "This bus will take you to the bus stop near your home." Before I could voice my thanks, he disappeared. I never saw him again. I believe he was an angel sent to guide me during this first day in a big city."

EDITOR'S COMMENT: One of the spirits that watched over Betty led this man or angel to her side in her time of need. Betty's spirit guides also sent her another helpful person in 1997, as explained in a following story.

BETTY'S STORY #3: ABOUT 1955 – A ROMAN SPIRIT VISITOR

Betty Bent told the following story: "One night, it was late when I was in the kitchen mopping the floor in my home in Compton, California. I often mopped the floors late as the job was impossible to do with 6 children underfoot. It was about 10:30 p.m. and I was finished mopping and ready to go to bed. As I was leaving the kitchen, a dim figure appeared in the corner cabinets standing in them as though they weren't even there."

"He appeared to be a Roman soldier with shoulder length, light brown, softly curling hair. He was wearing a short white sleeveless toga that draped across his left shoulder down to his waist diagonally and wrapped around his waist. From it hung two golden tassels. His sandals had leather thongs that laced up around his calves just below his knees. He didn't say anything but his face and demeanor were so kind and warm and were radiating warmth and peace. I was startled and didn't hesitate to leave the room. When I went into the bedroom I started undressing and I saw him there. I said (in my mind) 'I'm sorry to undress in front of you, but this is as private as I can get.' He disappeared and I went to bed."

"I was puzzled but not frightened by the experience. Was there a message for me? Was he encouraging me to keep going and keep doing the exhausting work of caring for my wonderful family? Maybe he was a lover from a past life?"

EDITOR'S COMMENT: Often a person with psychic ability will remember one of their past lives, and this person could, in fact, have been a lover of Betty's from a previous life.

BETTY'S STORY #4: SUMMER 1963 - HOSTING A MUSICAL SPIRIT

Betty Bent told the following story: "In the summer of 1963 my sister and I flew from our homes in California to our hometown to visit our parents. One warm, lazy afternoon my sister and I walked two blocks to Fourth Street where there was an antique shop in a former home."

"We browsed around and bought a few presents to take back to our favorite neighbors. The proprietress said, 'Here's a little old antique piano, do either of you play?' I said that I did and she invited me to sit down and play something. I sat down on the stool and immediately felt like I was dressed in an outfit from the Civil War time period. I seemed to have on a poke bonnet with wide ribbon tied under my chin with a big bow near one ear. My dress had a tight –fitting bodice and the skirt was gathered full over petticoats and a hoop skirt. I started to play and my fingers were playing the cutest little peppy tune. I was not playing; someone else was playing through my fingers. I asked my sister and the proprietress if they knew the song I was playing. Neither one of them knew, nor neither did I. I became frightened and stopped playing. I stood up and felt like myself again."

EDITOR'S COMMENT: Sometimes Earth-bound ghosts or spirits that still linger in a dwelling can obtain enough energy to influence actions or words of a person. Some instances of this are called "automatic writing" – when a person's hands are taken over by a spirit, and the spirit writes things down that the person isn't even aware of, or couldn't even know about. In this case, the ghost or spirit of the Civil War female piano player manipulated Betty into playing a song on the piano that the ghost played when she was alive. She also provided Betty with an insight as to what she enjoyed wearing while she was alive and playing during the 1860s.

BETTY'S STORY #5: 1966 - ANGELIC INTERVENTION

Betty Bent told the following story: "One day the girls in the office where I was working decided to go out to lunch. I volunteered to drive. So with five co-workers in my Ford Mustang we had lunch and a very good time."

"On the way back, I prayed silently for a safe trip. Enroute, there appeared in front of me a white sawhorse with a sign that said "Detour Lane Closed Ahead." I slammed on the brakes and the girls screamed. I looked back over my left shoulder to see if traffic would allow me to turn left into the correct lane (but I saw nothing). I was in shock and felt totally helpless."

"Then I had the feeling that four angels were lifting my car and setting it down in the proper lane, then disappeared. I drove ahead in the space provided for me as if nothing unusual had happened."

"Ever since this 'miracle' happened I have been grateful that all of our lives were saved. Did the angels come to save us when I emphatically asked God to give us a safe trip? The girls never knew that I felt like a helpless zombie when I couldn't see anything when I looked back, and I never told them."

EDITOR'S COMMENT: Everyone has a guardian angel and a spirit guide. For more information about spirit guides, I recommend reading books by James Van Praagh. Obviously Betty's guardian angel performed this miracle.

BETTY'S STORY #6: 1983 – ABILITIES RUN IN THE FAMILY

Betty Bent told the following story: "In 1983 or 1984 my brother died and his memorial service was held in a church in Sacramento, California, near his home. My sister and her family and I and my family flew there to attend the service. Our parents were now living in an apartment near our homes in Southern California."

"My parents were not capable physically of making the trip. When we returned to Southern California, we visited my mother and she told us about her experience with my brother. The time was 11:50 a.m. Our brother wanted his service to be at 12 noon so that his friends from work could attend. Mother said that exactly at 11:50 a.m. he appeared to her. He was an accomplished guitarist and said that he was going to play "Wildwood Flower" one of her favorite songs. After he played, he told her that he needed to go as they were waiting for him and the service was about to start. He went right through the door without opening it and he was gone."

(Note from Betty's son Richard Bent: "I attended the funeral service and was staying at the home of my deceased uncle and his wife. The next morning while I was in the shower, I heard a scream from my aunt. I threw on my clothes and rushed out to see what the problem was. My aunt was on the floor with the phone dangling from the wall. We helped her and she told us that Grandma had told her about my uncle coming into her apartment and playing a song and then leaving. My aunt had been shocked by the call.")

EDITOR'S COMMENT: Betty's mother's sighting and hearing the spirit of her brother is more proof that the ability to be contacted by spirits is genetic. Betty's son Richard has also had experiences. In addition, when people pass, their spirits usually stay around to see who came to their wake. It's no surprise that Betty's brother went to visit his mother before he passed into the light. Usually after a wake, a spirit will then pass into the light.

BETTY'S STORY #7: 1997 SPIRITS INTERVENE TO PROVIDE HELP

Betty Bent told the following story: "I was taking my seriously ill husband back home from a doctor's visit. We had just moved so we could be closer to family and I was not very familiar with the area. I kept trying to find my way home without success. I started to panic and once again called out to God in a loud voice, 'God, please help me.'"

"Just then, as I was stopped at stop sign, a lady in the car next to me indicated to me to roll down my window. She said, 'I'm glad you are here. I didn't know you had moved.' I said, 'I'm lost and I don't know if I'm glad I'm here.' She got out of her car, not minding the traffic, and said to me, 'follow me' and she guided us home. She said that she had recognized my unique license plate. She and her husband were friends of my son Richard and had been to our home in Redondo Beach when we lived there. She was sent to me as an angel to guide us home."

EDITOR'S COMMENT: There is no such thing as a coincidence. One of the spirits that watched over Betty led this friend of her son's to her side in her time of need. The same thing happened when my father passed in August 2009. Someone who was a complete stranger in the parking lot where my dad collapsed answered my mother's screams for help. Oddly, the woman knew my older brother and his phone number, although my dad collapsed several cities away from where my brother lives.

Following are stories as told by Betty's son Richard, documenting his experiences.

RICHARD'S STORY #1: 1963: GHOSTLY VISITOR CONFIRMED YEARS LATER

Richard Bent told the following story: "My aunt and uncle had been asked by a relative to close out a ranch property in the foothills of the San Bernardino Mountains of California. My aunt's uncle had died and left a rather large estate with lots of his personal property that needed to be sold off. My family and I had been invited to spend Easter week with them at the ranch. The ranch house was a turn of the century Victorian/farmhouse style. It was white and had several rooms filled with his possessions, which included old appliances, Victrolas (old stereos that played the original vinyl records), 78 rpm records and his old suits that still hung in the closet. The house was on a property of at least 200 acres, and it had a small lake and barns which housed old vehicles."

"The second or third night we were there, it was very cold and windy. I slept in a room with my cousin on the second floor, I believe. I remember not being asleep long when I was woken up by the sound of the tree branches striking the window of the room we were sleeping in. My imagination ran wild, and I got scared. At one point in the night I got a sense of a large man in a double-breasted suit in my room. I was so scared, but then I thought it was my overactive imagination. I eventually got to sleep. I said nothing of it."

"About 8 or 9 years later, my uncle called our house and I heard my mother conversing with him over the phone. When she was finished she came back to the kitchen table and told us they were talking about our visit to the ranch several years earlier. One of the items she mentioned was that the second night we were there both my uncle and his wife had the sensation of the former owner being in the vicinity. When I heard this I let out some kind of surprising sound and explained to those present that I had also experienced this, and it was not my imagination."

EDITOR'S NOTE: Obviously, Richard's family members have the ability to see and sense spirits. Even his uncle has the ability. Richard's family is proof that the ability to sense and communicate with spirits is genetic.

RICHARD'S STORY #2: 1986: A SPIRIT'S INFLUENCE

"My wife and I had driven up to Gold Country east of Sacramento, California, to go on a river rafting trip. This was the area where my deceased uncle had spent a lot of his recreation time in his Jeep traveling the back roads. As mentioned in a previous story, he was an accomplished guitarist and adapted many songs to a folk, picking style. He used to play the song "My Grandfather's Clock" quite often at family get-togethers. It was a very complicated piece but he played it beautifully."

"As we were unpacking the car in the campground, my wife began to whistle the song, 'My Grandfather's Clock.' This could have been coincidence, but I was not aware of my wife ever hearing my uncle play that song. She had never hummed or sang it before and lastly, she doesn't whistle! When I asked what she was doing, she looked up surprised, stopped whistling and said, "I don't know." Then she said, Uncle Willy is paying a visit. She didn't know that this was his stomping ground."

EDITOR'S COMMENT: Sometimes spirits will influence people to make decisions or behave or say something to help remind a person of them and to let them know that they're around. Such was the case with Richard's uncle's spirit influencing his wife to whistle his favorite tune from when he was alive.

RICHARD'S STORY #3: 2008: AN ELECTRIC MANIPULATION

"While sitting alone in our family room late one night, I was contemplating turning the TV off when to my utter amazement, the lights in the room connected to a dimmer suddenly got very bright. I was several feet from the switch and everyone else was asleep when this happened. I was a bit unnerved."

EDITOR'S COMMENT: As mentioned in Chapter 2, electricity is one way in which spirits can communicate with the living. Spirits are often known to affect electric current.

RICHARD'S STORY #4: 2008: SPIRITS USING WATER TO CONVEY A MESSAGE

"The Pierpont Inn was built in 1910 and is situated on the California coast. Josephine Pierpont commissioned a famous architect at the time, Sumner P. Hunt, to design the inn."

"While visiting the Pierpont Inn at 550 San Jon Road, Ventura, California, earlier this year, we learned about a female spirit who wandered the grounds. When my wife had gone to bed, I wandered around the grounds at night looking for a sign of this spirit. I went to an un-restored part of the Inn and sat and listened. After a time, I gave up and went back to our room."

"The next morning while taking a shower, the water suddenly went off. I thought perhaps it was a maintenance problem, but then I noticed that the knobs were in the off position. The realization hit me that something or someone must have done that. I decided I was clean enough and got out of there quickly."

EDITOR'S COMMENT: In addition to electricity, spirits can also manifest themselves by utilizing the energy from running water. I've experienced messages in the shower and walking around in towns like Ellicott City, Maryland, that have rivers running through or near them.

CHAPTER 19
Ghost/Spirit Stories From Others: Part Two

The rest of this chapter is devoted to encounters that other friends, colleagues or acquaintances have had with spirits, or strange phenomena. It is alphabetized by the U.S. state in which the event occurred. All of these were freely submitted to me for publication in this book.

ALABAMA

LEAH IN TUSCUMBIA: A FRIEND'S GRANDFATHER APPEARS IN HIS FORMER HOUSE

In a letter from May, 2009 Leah P. wrote: "I have been meaning to write to tell you my semi-recent encounter with a ghost. On January 2, 2009, I went to visit my friend Jessica in Tuscumbia, Alabama. She is a huge Alabama football fan, and that night they were playing in the Sugarbowl."

"The game was on TV, and I was sitting on the daybed. Jessica was in the kitchen. I looked over toward the TV, and there was a man sitting in the chair looking at the TV! Jessica came into the doorway, and I said, 'Jessica, there was a man sitting in the chair a second ago!'"

"I told her what he looked like, and she said, 'That was probably my grand-daddy. He loved football.' The old house was his house before Jessica lived in it."

"I was not in the least bit frightened. I got goose bumps when Jessica said who it was, though. I saw him as clear as day. Jess said that she has heard noises and seen someone going back and forth in the kitchen before. Pretty darn cool!"

EDITOR'S COMMENT: It's not uncommon for spirits to come back to places where they lived or felt most comfortable. Obviously, Jessica's grand-daddy loved his house and loved watching football. Every now and then he apparently comes back to enjoy a game with his grand-daughter.

KENTUCKY

KERRY AND TOM'S EXPERIENCES IN BOWLING GREEN: APPORTS AND A VISIBLE GHOST

When I lived in Bowling Green, Kentucky in 1996, not only was the house I lived in haunted, but two friends that lived in an old downtown Bowling Green three-story home also had a haunting, and a very active one.

My friends Kerry and Tom lived in a makeshift apartment that took up the entire top floor of an old three-story building. The building was built in the 1800s and looked like an old hotel of sorts. I wouldn't be surprised if it was hotel at one time, as there were so many bedrooms in it. On the top floor alone, there were four bedrooms, although Kerry and Tom only used two of them. All of the bedrooms were on the left side of the house and were connected by a long hallway that extended from the back to the front of the house. Their kitchen was on the right side of the house, and their living room was in the front of the house at one end of the hallway. The layout of the house is important to these stories.

When I first mentioned to Kerry and Tom that I knew I had a ghost around the house I was living in (one that kept banging on the outside door at 2:30 a.m. and not triggering the sensor light), they shared their stories with me.

Kerry told me that a number of times he would come home, set his mail down in the living room and come back for it later. Often, he said, he would find things missing from where he put them, only to reappear in the exact same place later. He couldn't explain it, but it was an apport happening.

One evening in the spring of 1997, Kerry came home, opened his mail and laid down a paycheck on his living room table next to a lamp. He said he went into his bedroom and changed clothes and came back out. The check was missing. He called out for his roommate Tom, and then checked the house for him, thinking Tom had come home and hidden the check to be playful. Tom wasn't home.

Kerry said he searched for hours and couldn't imagine what happened to the check. He said he got frustrated and called out "Okay, ghost, I know you took my paycheck and I really need it! Now put it back!" When he came back in the living room, the check was exactly where he placed it originally.

Another story Kerry and Tom told me involved a door down a back stairway that was nailed shut. Several times, they came home and found the door open. However, when it was closed, they couldn't budge it.

The third story happened when I was on the phone one day in early 1997 with Tom. Kerry wasn't home. Tom was in his bedroom, which was located in the far back bedroom, and talking to me on a portable phone. Tom said that he heard something down in Kerry's bedroom, which was located at the other end of the hallway, just before the entrance into the living room. So, Tom walked down the hallway with the portable phone.

He called for Kerry as he walked down the hallway, and I was listening. No answer. When he got to Kerry's room, he screamed and the phone went dead. I called back immediately, and he had run downstairs to the outside of the house.

Tom said that in the corner of Kerry's darkened room, there was a Confederate soldier standing by Kerry's bed, dressed in full uniform. The soldier scared the hell out of Tom. Of course, now they knew who was causing the apports, and moving things around the house.

EDITOR'S NOTE: That house was full of paranormal activity, from apports to apparitions. The ghost in the house also used a lot of energy to open a door that was nailed shut. Obviously the ghost wanted to continue using that entrance/exit as it had when it was alive.

KENTUCKY

JEFF E., BOWLING GREEN: AN AUDIBLE GHOST, AND ELECTRIC MANIPULATION

In an email on June 8, 2005, Jeff told the following story: "I had two friends that lived next door to one another in Bowling Green, Kentucky. They claimed that their houses were both haunted. At the very least, they claimed there was definitely strange activity going on. I, of course, did not believe them. Behind their homes was a small family graveyard containing three sisters who were allegedly witches. The three sisters died in a house fire that started from suspicious circumstances."

"One afternoon after talking with my friend Randy on my cell phone, he told me to wait at his house for him. So, I went to my friend Randy's house, which was located in the subdivision of Hidden River Estates, and I let myself inside where I fell asleep on his couch. I was startled awake by someone yelling my name from a very close proximity. I thought it was Randy. I immediately jumped up and ran down the hall in the hopes of catching him hiding. There was no one there but me. Just as I came to the realization that I was still alone in the house, the radio alarm clock in Randy's bedroom came on, blaring. I went in and turned it off. I simply played everything off as coincidence."

"The yelling of my name could have been a dream, and the radio alarm coming on could have been simply that the alarm had been set incorrectly. Here's where it gets weird. A few weeks later, I was at the same house. I had not told Randy about my experience. We were sitting on the couch and Randy began to tell me about a strange occurrence. He said that he had fallen asleep on the couch and was awakened by someone yelling his name very loudly and from close range. He said that it sounded like me, but that he jumped to his feet and ran down the hall to "catch" me. There was no one there. That made the hair on the back of my neck stand up. I took it upon myself to relay my story to Randy. Just as I finished my story the radio alarm clock in his room came on blaring again. We both laughed, and he said that he was going to take a shower."

"He went into the shower and I turned his clock radio off. When I got back to the living room, the radio came on again. This time I unplugged the radio alarm. As I was settling into my chair in the living room, the radio alarm in his son's upstairs bedroom came on. That is when every hair on my body stood at attention. I went up and turned off the radio. No logical explanation could be reached."

EDITOR'S COMMENT: For a spirit or ghost to actually be heard by human ears without use of an EVP is a signal of a very strong-willed ghost or spirit. The usage of electricity (turning the alarm clock on) is just one way spirits and ghosts communicate. Water is another, so I asked Jeff about the location of the house, and wanted to know if there was any water nearby, as moving water enables spirits to manifest themselves (such as the case of the very haunted Ellicott City, Maryland, mentioned elsewhere in this book). He said behind his friend's house, there was a cave about 75 to 100 yards away. In the cave, there was an underground river, possibly associated with the famous Lost River Chain. Lost River is in the Guinness Book of world records. The Lost River is the shortest, deepest river in the world. It is above ground for only about 200 yards but the depths of the river have been measured at between 400 and 500 feet. It's right there in Bowling Green, Kentucky.

MAINE

RICK R., PORTLAND MAINE: VISIBLE GHOST, ELECTRICITY MANIPULATION

"Bob Anderson, who was known in the area as 'The Duke of Portland,' was the morning announcer on Oldies 100.9 FM radio in Portland, Maine, for many years. Just before America went to war with Iraq, it was decided to have all the morning shows live that Saturday, in case war did break out and the station had to broadcast the news. While at the radio station that morning, Bob suffered a heart attack and died with his microphone on just before he was going to do a commercial break."

"If it had been any other Saturday, Bob would have died at home, and since he lived alone, it could have been days before he was found. But, because of special circumstances, Bob died doing what he loved most."

"One night, Jaime, a woman who was manning the station in the overnights, saw someone run past her studio window. Since you can't get in the building without knowing the password to a combination punch lock, she knew it was someone who was supposed to be there, so she wasn't overly worried and went to find the person to introduce herself. She didn't find him anywhere. She mentioned it to one of the other announcers, who showed her a picture of Bob on the wall in the Oldies studio. 'That was who I saw!' she insisted."

"A few nights later, she was sitting in the sister station, WMGX 93.1FM, studio (in the same building as Oldies 100.9 FM) when the microphone kept turning on and off for no reason whatsoever, and she couldn't figure out why. Finally, she calmly said: 'Is that you, Bob?' The microphone clicked on and off again. 'I hear that you were a really nice guy,' she said, 'and I'm sure you're just saying 'hi' to welcome me to the radio station, and I really appreciate that, and 'hi' to you as well, but you're really freaking me out, so could you please not do that anymore?' She tells me that as soon as she said that, the microphone stopped clicking, and did not do it again."

"Several of the people who work there, though, are sure Bob's ghost is wandering the halls of the radio station, since it was where he liked being more than anywhere else when he was alive. In fact, that was the reason the other announcer had shown Jaime that photo. He was sure she had seen Bob."

EDITOR'S COMMENT: Spirits who have passed into the light will sometimes come back to a place where they were most comfortable in life, as "Bob" came back to the radio station where he felt at home. Earth-bound ghosts will also continue to linger in a place they were attached to. As in the previous story, this spirit manipulated electricity by turning the microphone off and on, to let someone know the spirit was still enjoying being at work.

MARYLAND

JENNIFER N.: STORY #1: APPORTS

In May 2009, Jennifer N. wrote: "I have been interested in ghosts and the paranormal as long as I can remember...back into the middle elementary school years. In fact, when I was 10, I know I had already decided that being a 'ghost hunter' was one of the things I thought I'd want to 'be' when I grew up...I remember writing about it in a school assignment. I know that at the age of 8 or 9 my mother started to worry about me because I loved to read books about mythological monsters, werewolves and ghosts. She was a worrier."

"I'm not sure what originally sparked my interest, but I can tell you that my stepfather (who has been in my life since the age of three) has had a lifelong career as a funeral director, at one time was the owner of three funeral homes, and is even now in retirement the general manager of a large cemetery. So, from a young age I was exposed to more talk about death than the average kid! I remember experiencing a feeling of panic as a little girl regarding aspects of death, the inevitability of it, the 'foreverness' of it, and the awful possibility that there might be nothing on the other side. I was raised in the Methodist church, so I was taught about heaven and hell, but I've always been a person who has wondered and questioned, even as a kid, and maybe not always out loud."

"I think I am often pretty sensitive to the atmospheres of places; however, there have been three times that I can remember when things have happened to me that were definitely strange, seemed to have no logical explanation, and may have been paranormal."

"When I was a teenager and young adult, I worked at a conference center in my hometown, which was a large house built in 1732, on 80 acres of its original estate. This place was magical...a great place to work, with great people who were like a family. This house has a long history of ghost activity. It seems that nearly everyone who has worked there has had some kind of strange experience."

"I worked in many departments during the 10 years I was there, from housekeeping to management....always felt safe and welcome, despite the fact that I very often felt I wasn't alone, when there wasn't another living person with me."

"One evening when I was in college, during the time that I was working as a waitress, I was alone in the dining room after all the guests had finished eating, clearing the tables. The dining room was the house's original kitchen....large enough to seat about 30 people. There were two large windows on each of the east and west walls and a large original fireplace on the north wall. In the center hung a brass chandelier which I believe was original to the house. The chef was cleaning the kitchen, and the other waitress was washing dishes. There was a closed door between me and the kitchen and another closed door between the dining room and the rest of the house. I was busy clearing the tables, stacking dishes into a tub sitting on one of the chairs, when behind me I heard a 'thump' and turned around in time to see a large black olive falling from the direction of the wall, high up near the ceiling, as if someone had thrown it!"

"We would serve a dish of olives at each table during dinner, large black olives which still contained pits. As you can imagine there were often several left in the dish at the end of a meal."

"As I said, both doors were closed and I was alone...a wee bit shaken, I went into the kitchen to see what everyone was doing...both of my coworkers were absorbed in their tasks and clearly hadn't had time to sneak out, scare me, and race back to look casual. There was nothing for me to do but go back to the dining room and finish my work, alone with that creepy feeling!"

"I continued to clear tables. I was in the center of the room, directly under the old chandelier, when another olive fell from directly above me.....a direction where clearly no person could be! Now I was slightly alarmed and went back into the kitchen to tell everyone what had happened. I really was pretty excited that finally, the ghost seemed to have made contact with me personally."

EDITOR'S NOTE: An apport means to move an object from one place to another. It's one form of communication that Earth-bound ghosts or spirits use. In this case whoever was haunting this old house, and most likely it was a ghost that either lived there before or frequented the place, used olives to send Jennifer a message that it was their place. In intelligent haunts, ghosts will also throw items or slam doors to send a signal that they want their premises to be left alone.

MARYLAND

JENNIFER N.: STORY #2: AUDIBLE FOOTSTEPS AND A PEACEFUL ENDING

Jennifer N. wrote: "About 8 years after the apport incident, I was married and the mother of a small child. My husband and I moved to a tiny town on the Eastern Shore (of Maryland) on the Chesapeake Bay, which had been a steamboat resort from about the turn of the century until about the 1950s."

"We lived in a house originally built as a summer cottage. The second floor had two bedrooms opening onto the hall, which also had a door which connected the two rooms. One room belonged to us, and the other to our little girl; we never used the connecting door, and in fact, we had furniture placed in front of it on one or both sides."

"Occasionally, I would be sitting in the living room below and hear very distinct footsteps moving above, from one bedroom to the next, all the way across the house....seeming to pass through the adjoining door. Other people sometimes heard these too, sometimes at the same time as me and sometimes when they were alone. My mother heard it repeatedly, the night she stayed with my daughter when my husband and I were at the hospital waiting for our youngest daughter to be born."

"We have neighbors whose house is very close to ours, about 12-15 feet away. While we can hear noises from their house, they never sound as if they are coming from within our house, as these footsteps did. We haven't heard these steps for many years now---at least not since we converted the attic into a master bedroom and the second floor rooms became rooms for our daughters. I don't really know anything about our house other than that it was built in 1930 by a man named Owens. He still has descendants in the area, one of whom has even done some work on our house. The land our house was built on was (in the 19th century and maybe earlier) once a farm."

EDITOR'S NOTE: Earth-bound ghosts that are still wandering in a home or place can be heard as they "walk around." Ghosts who don't understand that they are no longer among the living and that another family lives in their former home sometimes don't want to share the residence, so they make themselves known trying to get the new family to leave. Sometimes Earth-bound ghosts don't like what the new residents are doing to "their home" and make themselves known in various ways. However, if they do like any new renovations, sometimes they will quiet down and live together peacefully or leave of their own accord.

In the instance where ghosts are walking through the once-used doorway, now blocked with furniture, it is because that's where they walked when they were alive; just as in one of the previous stories, where Kerry and Tom's ghost kept opening the door that was nailed closed. The ghost was used to going through it during its life on Earth, so it continues to do so even in death.

The ghost in this story, however, doesn't seem to be an intelligent haunt where the ghost can interact with the living. Rather, this ghost seems to be repeating what it did during its lifetime.

MASSACHUSETTS

MAUREEN C., NORFOLK: SPIRITS CAN COMMUNICATE WHILE YOU SLEEP, OR THROUGH OTHERS

Maureen wrote in 2005: "Our family lives in the house that I grew up in with my parents and two brothers. My two older boys, Vinny and Nick, now share a bedroom that was once my parents' bedroom. One evening a few years back, I was watching a pre-taped Oprah Winfrey show in my bedroom late at night."

"My husband was not home at the time, and the boys were asleep in their bedroom. I believe that Oprah's show had psychic medium John Edwards as the guest. He was talking about how the "other side" reaches out to us all the time. I found the show very interesting and was moved to tears thinking about my both my mother and my grandmother, both of whom had passed away within two months of each other when I was pregnant with my first child, Vinny."

"When the show was over, I shut off the TV and was heading to the bathroom to wash up. I then heard a noise from the boys' room. I opened the door, and there was Vinny lying in his bed, eyes wide open, yet sound asleep. He began to talk to me telling me that everything was going to be alright and that 'they' were fine and not to worry or cry for 'them.'"

"I don't know if the show I was watching about people in the next life had anything to do with the timing of Vinny's message or not. Vinny was only 10 at the time and does not remember anything that he had said to me that evening. After that, I felt more at peace knowing that my mom and grandmother were okay, and I felt their presence that night like I never did before."

EDITOR'S COMMENT: The easiest way for spirits to communicate with us is through our dreams when we're sleeping. That's the time that our logical minds are at rest. It's our logical minds that actually block spirits from communicating with us. When we're asleep, our minds are open and allow messages to come through. Sometimes, as in this case, a spirit can communicate through one person to provide a message to another, whether the person being channeled through is awake or asleep. It was no coincidence that Maureen had watched the program with the medium the night that messages came through for her. Obviously, Maureen's mother and grandmother saw that night as the perfect opportunity to communicate with her because her mind was open to it.

JANICE P., NANTUCKET: MOVING OBJECTS, NOISES

In September 2008, my friend Janice from Nantucket, Massachusetts, wrote: "I think my former boss came for a visit."

"A weird thing just happened to me at work, and I think it might be ghost related. I had Monday and Tuesday off and came into work this morning and sat down at my desk. I began to start in on some paperwork and reached for my date stamp to set it to today's date."

"When I checked the date I was VERY surprised to see it had already been set to today's date – Wednesday, September 3rd. I mentioned it to my officemate Laura, and she told me she had a strange experience in the office yesterday. She came in at 8 a.m. as usual and heard papers rustling on the other side of the room divider. Thinking it was me, she said 'Good morning' (I usually come in at 7:30 a.m., so I am at my desk on other side of the partition when she arrives)."

"The noise continued but she did not receive a reply and thought perhaps I was having a bad morning or was on the phone. After a minute or two, realizing I still hadn't acknowledged her, she came around the partition only to find an empty desk, no one there. However, she noticed that one of my desk drawers was open."

"There is only one door to our office, and we are on the second floor of the hospital. There was no way someone could have been at my desk and left without Laura seeing them."

"After she told me about her experience, I remembered that yesterday was the 9th anniversary of my friend and former boss' passing. Our department Manager Kathi passed away Labor Day weekend 1999. She was one of the most hard-working bosses I have ever had. I thought that it would be so much like Kathi to step in and do some work or change the date on my stamp when I was off. I can't help but think that she stopped by to check on things were going."

MISSISSIPPI

CHARLES J.: AN AUDIBLE SIGN

Charles wrote: "It is hard for me to believe that someone can return from the dead. The thought of it nearly makes the hair on the back of my neck stand up! This background thinking came from the religious teachings I learned while growing up. I was taught that when a person dies, the body returns to the earth, the spirit returns to God, and the soul goes to the Haden World while waiting for the Judgment Day (Example: The Rich Man and Lazarus; Luke 16: 19-31)."

"Fortunately I've only had one experience in my life that is unexplainable. When I was in high school one night I was lying down in my parents' bedroom in the dark resting. I heard a breathing sound, but there was no one else in the room. I held my breath just to make sure that I wasn't hearing my own breathing. It wasn't. The breathing continued. I tried to remain calm. When I got my courage up, I turned on the light but didn't see anyone else in the room."

NEW HAMPSHIRE AND PENNSYLVANIA (One person's experiences)

JIM K., MANCHESTER, NH: STORY #1: AN APPARITION

Jim wrote in June 2005: My first supernatural experience happened in December 1972, when I was a boy in Bethel Park, Pennsylvania. That's located in the suburbs of Pittsburgh. It was about a month after my grandfather passed away.

As a kid, I shared a bedroom with one of my brothers. I remember lying awake in my bed while my brother was sleeping. It was late at night, and everyone had gone to sleep. I glanced toward the open door of my bedroom, which gave me a view of the stairs. I remember seeing a figure "walk" up the stairs. The figure appeared to be looking around. It glanced into our bedroom, but it didn't look right at me, though, sort of just into the room. Then the figure turned and looked straight ahead into my other brother's room. Then it turned and looked down the hallway. I then saw it "walk" away towards my parents' room.

I fell asleep shortly afterwards, feeling very safe and secure. To this day I feel that I had seen my grandfather's ghost checking in on us, making sure that we were okay and letting us know that he was watching over us.

EDITOR'S COMMENT: Sometimes when the spirit of a deceased relative returns, a person will feel a sense of peace.

JIM K., MANCHESTER, NH: STORY #2: AN APPARITION, COLD SPOTS

Jim wrote: "My next experience occurred near Silver Lake in Hollis, New Hampshire. It was in the fall of 1996. I bought a house in Hollis and moved in, bringing my elderly mother with me. At that time, it had been two years since my dad passed away."

"The house had a very large family room at one end of the house, and the kitchen, bathroom and laundry room at the other end of the house. Directly across from the bathroom was our living room."

"My mother and I were watching TV in the family room. I remember glancing into the kitchen when I saw a shadowy figure walk from the living room to the bathroom. The figure walked the way my dad used to walk. What struck me about this is that the small hallway from the living room to the bathroom was not lit very well. Yet the figure appeared 'darker' than the surrounding area. It wasn't 100% black, but sort of dark blue/purple/black. I got up and went down to the bathroom. Of course, no one was there."

"The living room and bathroom felt cooler than the rest of the kitchen. From time to time mom and I would hear the steps creak as if someone was walking up them to the second floor. But the ghostly figure was the only apparition that I saw. I knew for sure it was my dad. I never told mom, as it probably would have upset her."

EDITOR'S COMMENT: Spirits who have crossed (or even Earth-bound ghosts) can come back and make themselves visible. Sometimes they can appear as they did when they were living; other times they will appear as a shadow. What reinforced Jim's sight of his father's spirit was the cold in the rooms. Spirits draw heat and electric energy to manifest themselves and leave behind cooler temperatures.

JIM K., MANCHESTER, NH: STORY #3: DOGS SENSING SPIRITS, COLD SPOTS

Jim wrote: "My next experience was in Hudson, New Hampshire, located near the west end of Manchester, New Hampshire, where I had moved after living in Hollis."

"Now this is really weird. It was in 2001. My partner and I and our dog Bacardi had moved into our "new" house, and my elderly mother moved into one of our guest rooms."

"Along the hallway in the house, we hung four paintings that had belonged to my paternal grandmother. I still have the paintings. These paintings are very small, about 6"x4" and are oil painted on wood. They were done by Carl Roth in 1939. I only know that because the artist put his label on the back of each painting and signed each one of them."

"One night when it was time to turn in, my mother had already gone to her room. I was already in my bed, and my partner was walking down the hall. When he reached the bedroom our dog Bacardi was lying in the doorway between our bedroom and the hallway. My partner told Bacardi to move, and Bacardi got up and walked into the hallway. Ed came into the bedroom."

"The next thing we knew Bacardi sat down in front of the paintings, looked up at them and started barking. Not a playful bark, but a serious bark. He just sat there barking at the paintings. This went on for about 30 seconds, then my partner yelled at him to stop, and he did. I sat right up in bed, the hairs on the back of my neck stood up also! As he was barking, I felt a cold breeze move through me. The whole scene freaked me out, but I remained calm."

"I never told my partner about the cold breeze, as he just doesn't believe in these things. I still do not know what or who Bacardi was barking at but something was definitely there."

EDITOR'S COMMENT: Sometimes ghosts or spirits will attach their energies to objects that they loved during their time on Earth. As mentioned, I've sensed energies attached to a number of pieces of furniture in antique stores, and even an old mattress that we had. Apparently, either Jim's grandmother or the painter's energies were still attached to those paintings, and their dog, Bacardi sensed it. It was most likely a residual haunting, meaning that it's leftover energy from "emotion" or "love of the object" that was attached to the paintings. Dogs, like children (who are open minded), have a much easier time seeing spirits because their minds aren't clouded with "logical thinking."

JIM K., MANCHESTER, NH: STORY #4: HIS DOG SEES HIS MOTHER'S SPIRIT

Jim wrote: "Finally, there are two episodes that had taken place at our home since my Mom passed away. First, I was downstairs in our basement doing the laundry and our dog Bacardi was with me. Many of my mom's pieces of furniture and belongings were stored down in the basement after she passed."

"While doing the laundry, I turned to see what the dog was doing. This freaked me out. Bacardi was standing still, looking straight at my mom's stuff. His head was cocked to one side, and he was slowly wagging his tail, in a friendly, but not quite friendly way. He just stood there doing that for 5 minutes. I just froze. I didn't see anything, hear anything, smell anything or feel anything. Bacardi though definitely saw something."

"I've caught Bacardi doing this in other places throughout the house, such as staring into a corner. What does he see?"

EDITOR'S COMMENT: Jim's dog Bacardi was obviously looking right at the spirit of Jim's mother in the basement (and in other locations in the house).

JIM K., MANCHESTER, NH: STORY #5: ELECTRIC MANIPULATION

Jim wrote: "The second episode involved my partner's nightstand lamp. This lamp can only be turned on by touching it. There are no switches, and your touch completes the circuit. The wiring on the lamp was okay as well as the lights."

"After my mother passed, on occasion, when we would come home or go upstairs to the bedroom, we would find the light turned on. Many times I thought my partner forgot to turn it off. But several times we have both left the room, with the light off, only to return later (usually when it's time for bed) and the light was on!"

"I've tried to see if when the furnace turned on if it somehow trips the light on, but to no avail. I also checked to see if the drapes would brush against it and turn it on when the warm or cold air blows into the room. It doesn't reach."

"I concluded that the only way for the light to turn on is for someone to touch it. So, how does it turn on then, when nobody is in the house except for our dog Bacardi, who is always in his crate when we go out?"

"My partner and I have jokingly said that "the ghost" has turned the light on again. I truly feel, though, it is my mom, just making sure that we're safe."

"So yeah, I believe in ghosts. Not necessarily the mean ones, but ghosts of loved ones who, now and then, stop by to make sure we're doing okay."

EDITOR'S NOTE: Electricity is one of the main things that ghosts and spirits can manipulate because they are forms of energy. It was obviously Jim's mother leaving the light on for them and letting him know that she's still watching over them.

NORTH CAROLINA

CHARLOTTE IN JAMESTOWN: SCENT REMINDER
Charlotte told me that since her former boyfriend, Bob, passed, she has on occasion smelled his "Old Spice" aftershave.

EDITOR'S NOTE: Sometimes spirits who have passed can recreate scents that were connected with them during their time on Earth. I've heard of accounts of scents of roses where female spirits once loved living and strong new smells of a cigar or cigarette that mysteriously appears in a place where there is no one smoking.

TENNESSEE

RON B., NASHVILLE, TN: STORY #1: PHYSICAL CONTACT WITH A SPIRIT
Ron titled his ghost stories, "The Ghosts of Studio B." He wrote: "The Country Music Hall of Fame and Music, where I worked as a weekend supervisor in the Visitor Services Department, offers guided tours of RCA Studio B, the oldest surviving recording studio in Nashville. One of my responsibilities included promoting the tours of RCA Studio B, so over the past several years I have become very familiar with the building and its history."

"*GRAMMY Magazine* has stated, 'Based on sheer hit output, RCA Studio B is arguably the most successful studio of all time. In the 20 years from its opening in 1957 to its closing on August 17, 1977 – the day after Elvis's death – Studio B was home to 16,000 separate sessions which produced 47,000 individual songs, of which over 1,000 became Top 10 hit singles.'"

"Elvis is undoubtedly the most famous artist to record at Studio B, and he made over 250 recordings there. His first session was on June 10, 1958. Exactly 13 years to the day later – on June 10, 1971 – Elvis made his last recordings, which included 'My Way,' at Studio B."

"The 1960 "Solid Gold" Cadillac on display at the Country Music Hall of Fame and Museum was used by Elvis to travel between his Graceland home in Memphis and RCA Studio B in Nashville. A year before he died, Elvis donated the car to the museum, driving the car himself from RCA Studio B to the museum's former location on Music Row."

"Many visitors to Studio B have claimed they have experienced the spirit or ghost of Elvis within the studio's walls. Following one of the guided tours, I remember a young woman from England was having her photo taken at the same microphone podium that Elvis used. All of a sudden the woman started shaking and she had to be taken to a chair to sit down and regain her composure. Tears came to her eyes as she tried to explain what had happened. She said that she felt the presence of a man putting his arm around her shoulder as she was standing at Elvis's podium."

EDITOR'S COMMENT: A spirit can manifest itself enough to actually be felt. It takes a lot of energy for a spirit to do that, if not electric or water energy, a spirit can utilize emotional energy, such as excitement or nervousness.

RON B., NASHVILLE: STORY #2: SPIRIT ATTACHMENTS TO INANIMATE OBJECTS

"There is a well-known story, confirmed by several studio musicians, that says during one recording session Elvis kicked the side of a wooden cabinet which held a record player that was used to play acetate demos. Elvis's kick knocked loose a portion of the wooden cabinet door. Over the years several attempts were made to repair the cabinet, but the broken piece of the door continued to fall off. To this day, visitors on the guided tour can still see the broken door."

EDITOR'S NOTE: Spirits or energy from spirits can attach themselves to pieces of furniture or belongings that they had during their time on Earth. Sometimes, like when people renovate homes where an Earth-bound ghost still exists, the entity or energy that is attached to the inanimate object doesn't want it altered from the way they left it. Such was the case with Elvis' broken cabinet. He left it that way and wanted it to stay that way, so his energy keeps returning it to the way he left it. Regarding the haunted rooms, there are stories where furniture is found placed back into its original position, even after a new owner has moved it.

RON B., NASHVILLE: STORY #3: A FAMOUS SPIRIT

"One of my favorite artists and personalities in country music was the late Dottie West, who also recorded at Studio B. Dottie had spunk and fire and a heart of gold. She was also one of the best friends of one of my best friends, Grand Ole Opry member Jeannie Seely."

"Dottie had a reputation of running late, and Friday, August 30, 1991, was no exception. Dottie was scheduled to sing on the 8:30 p.m. portion of the Grand Ole Opry. About 8:00 p.m. Dottie headed out, but her car, a Chrysler New Yorker that Kenny Rogers had given her, stalled out in front of the old Belle Meade Theatre on Harding Road. A neighbor from Wessex Towers, where Dottie was living, offered her a ride to the Opry."

"The 81-year-old driver didn't slow down and lost control on the Briley Parkway exit into the Opryland Theme Park. At 8:11 p.m. his car left the road and went over 180 feet across the grass, then struck an embankment of the ramp, went almost 100 feet in the air, and then struck the ground. Not knowing the extent of her injuries, Dottie pulled the neighbor from the car, and when the ambulance arrived, she insisted he be taken to the hospital first."

"Dottie had a lacerated liver and a ruptured spleen that was removed Friday night. On Monday, surgeons did further major repairs to her liver, which continued to bleed because of deep, multiple tears during the accident. Doctors then decided Dottie would have to be operated on again – the third time in five days. Vanderbilt University doctor John Morris said, 'Dottie knew the severity of her injuries when she went into surgery. She was aware of the fact that she was pretty ill.'"

"Dottie's body couldn't handle the stress of another operation, and she died on Tuesday, September 4, 1991, at 9:43 a.m. The death of Dottie West shocked the country music community and her fans around the world."

"Dottie became the very first female artist to receive a Grammy Award with 1964's 'Here Comes My Baby,' which was recorded at RCA Studio B. The only known videotape of Studio B recordings is footage taken in 1963 by a local television station that features Eddy Arnold, Jim Reeves, and Dottie West. As shown in the video footage, a blanket was thrown across the coat rack in the back of the room to reduce any rattling noises that may have come from it during a recording."

"A few years ago on a Saturday morning, I left the Country Music Hall of Fame and Museum and drove to RCA Studio B, as it was my responsibility that day to open the studio and make sure everything was set for the first guided tour at 10:30 a.m. I arrived at the studio, turned off the alarm system and stood still for a moment, because I was positive I had heard a noise coming from inside the studio room itself. I distinctly remember that it sounded like heavy metal coat hangers rattling together."

"I entered the dimly light studio room and immediately received goose bumps. As I looked over into the corner where the wooden podium stood that singers had used during the sessions, a vivid image of a smiling Dottie West appeared in my mind."

"It's hard to describe the feeling I experienced that morning, but I continued to think about it, especially when I heard 'Here Comes My Baby' played later that same day."

"Epilogue: As I sat in the audience at Radio City Music Hall on August 18, 2005, a stranger sitting next to me began a friendly conversation while we both waited for Dolly Parton's show to begin. After a few minutes he said, 'I love all the duets that Dolly performed with Kenny Rogers, but I also love the duets he sang with Dottie West. She was absolutely one of my favorite entertainers.' Immediately – without even thinking about what I was going to say – I replied back, 'You could say that I wouldn't be sitting next to you right now if it wasn't for Dottie West.'"

"The stranger looked surprised, and he questioned what I meant by my statement. Because I had impulsively spoken the line, I had to stop and think about what I had just said. And then, as I had a flashback to my earlier experience in RCA Studio B, it hit me all of a sudden…and I explained it to him. It was Dottie West who recorded my friend Jeannie's song and encouraged her to move to Nashville… which Jeannie did. Then years later Jeannie encouraged me to move to Nashville… which I did. If Dottie hadn't befriended Jeannie and talked her into moving to Nashville, I wouldn't have moved there either. And if I hadn't moved to Nashville, I wouldn't be working for the company where I'm employed. And if I wasn't working for that company, I wouldn't have been in New York City, and if I hadn't been there I wouldn't have been attending the show at Radio City Music Hall."

EDITOR'S NOTE: The feeling that Ron had of Dottie West's presence was likely a sign from her. Most people are quick to dismiss feelings. You trust what you "hear" in your mind. It is only by trusting that you can verify what you've "heard." Additionally, we are all connected and those of us who are aware of connections understand that and how series of events come to pass – just like Ron's meeting the stranger at the concert who loved Dottie West.

CHAPTER 20
A Brief History of the Spiritual Movement

When I was writing this book, I wondered when it was that people and cultures became interested in ghosts and spirits. I've read stories about Native American and African cultures that involve spirits. Every culture seems to have some kind of shaman, oracle, witchdoctor, or someone that could provide warnings for the future or talk with someone on another plane to get that information.

When you think about it, even Jesus was a medium. He communicated with the spirits of Moses and Elijah on Mount Tabor, as it was later called in the fifth century. Moses and Elijah had passed into the light and came back to recognize Jesus as the "Son of God."

Three Gospels mention the event where Jesus is transfigured upon a mountain. They are Matthew 17:1-9, Mark 9:2-8 and Luke 9:28-36. During the event on the mountain top, Jesus became "radiant" or glowing, and he spoke with the spirits of Moses and Elijah. Three of the apostles were with Jesus on the mountain at the time: Peter, James and John. Another reference to ghosts came after Jesus' resurrection, when Christ appeared in a locked room surrounded by most of his disciples and said "I am not a ghost."

Jesus could also be considered as a psychic healer, but religions may dispute that. When you read stories in the Old and New Testaments from the Bible, there are a number of references to (psychic) healing, psychic abilities and even mediumship. Unfortunately, people who were mediums and "sorcerers" were later persecuted because of a ruling from the Council of Nicaea in the fourth century. They started an ancient witch hunt, similar to what happened later in Salem, Massachusetts, in the 1640s. There were implications and accusations that all mediums or psychics had relationships with the devil. They were then subject to death by torture, burning and other means after a "trial."

Times changed, and so did the church. It wasn't until 1995 that it became known that the Roman Catholic Church was carrying out scientific experiments with their own mediums! A Vatican theologian, Father Gino Concetti, wrote in the Pope's daily paper, 'Osservatore Romano,' the following: "According to the modern catechism the Church has decided not to forbid anymore to dialogue with the deceased ... this is as a sequel of new discoveries within the domain of the paranormal."

Ghosts and spirits have been part of many cultures around the world for centuries. Just do a search on the Internet, and you can find ghost and spirit stories from almost any country. Europe seems to be particularly haunted.

Even literature has been filled with references to ghosts, either real or fictional. Ghosts and spirits have been mentioned starting from the Bible, to classics like *Gilgamesh*, Shakespeare's "*Hamlet*," and Dickens' "*A Christmas Carol*."

All of the research I've done about the how spiritualism and mediumship came about puts the origin of the U.S. movement in the mid-1800s. Several sources place the birth of U.S. "spiritualism" in the 1840s. The main idea behind the movement was that mediums could communicate with the dead.

The first recorded historic account of a person or persons trying to communicate with ghosts or spirits occurred in 1848, where the Fox sisters actually contacted an Earth-bound ghost that was frightening a family by making sounds and being active in their home. It came to be known as the "Hydesville Knockings." The first public demonstration of mediumship occurred in 1849 by Margareta Fox in New York City, N.Y.

Today, thanks to technology, mediums and psychics can make themselves known to help others communicate with loved ones who have passed or Earth-bound ghosts that still linger. Mediums like James Van Praagh, John Edwards, Allison DuBois and many more are available to help.

Later, recording devices, photography and even Ouija boards (which I stay away from) were used in efforts to communicate with the dead. Today, ghost hunters still use digital recorders and different types of photography and video, such as infrared and visible light cameras. I personally steer clear of the Ouija boards, because you can accidentally "invite" a dark spirit into your home.

Attila von Szalay tried to record voices from beyond and was finally successful in 1956 using a reel-to-reel tape recorder. Three years later, Friedrich Jürgenson recorded songs of birds and heard what sounded like his late father's and late wife's voices on the tapes.

As technology progressed, so did the interest in recording spirit or Earth-bound ghost voices on tape. So, a woman named Sarah Estep of Maryland founded the American Association of Electronic Voice Phenomena in 1982. The purpose of the organization is to increase awareness and methods of using EVPs. See: *http://www.aaevp.com/*. The Web site offers examples, techniques and concepts concerning these phenomena. According to the AAEVP Web site, "EVP are anomalous, intelligible speech recorded in or produced by electronic devices, and for which no currently understood physical explanations can account."

Many organizations have sprung up and are available through a simple search on the Internet including mediums to psychics to scientific ghost hunters. To list them all would require another book in itself. One of the earliest organizations I found, however, started in 1901. It was called the Foundation of Spiritualists National Union Limited.

According to the Psychics and Mediums Web site (*http://www.psychics.co.uk/*) a number of books and organizations were published and founded from the mid-1800s on. Robert Owen wrote *The Principles of Spiritualism* in 1854, and a year later, Robert Hare wrote *Experimental Investigation of the Spirit Manifestation.* In 1856, Allen Kardec published his book, *'Le Livre des Esprits* (The Spirits' Book).

The last quarter century of the 1800s was booming with the creation of organizations that recognized supernatural phenomena. In 1875, the Theosophical Society was founded in New York City to investigate, study and explain mediumistic phenomena. Fifteen years later the National Spiritualists' Federation and the Spiritualists' Lyceum Union in England were founded. In 1893, the National Spiritualists Association of America was created.

In 1901 the Spiritualists National Union Limited was created. In 1932, the first issue of "Psychic News" was published. The British Broadcasting Corporation in England broadcast the first radio program about spirituality in 1934. In 1951 Eileen Garrett created the Parapsychology Foundation, based in New York City. The organization is still operational and can be found online at *http://www.parapsychology.org/.*

The Society for Psychical Research is a popular organization founded in the United Kingdom and is hosted over the Internet. For more information about the society, go to *www.spr.ac.uk/.* The society's Web page says that they were the first organization created that examines "allegedly paranormal phenomena using scientific principles." Their mission is to learn about events and abilities commonly described as "psychic" or "paranormal" through research, information sharing and debate. Because the society is Internet based, members can join from anywhere in the world and include professionals and the general public

As mentioned previously, The Atlantic Paranormal Society (TAPS), based in Warwick, Rhode Island, has brought ghost hunting into the realm of a hobby for people. It was founded in 1990 and became a hit television series in 2004 on the SyFy Channel.

TAPS accepts cases from the public and investigates free of charge. Their Web site states that all investigations are covered by their membership costs. Their Web site has a host of great reference materials from articles that include technology to an excellent glossary of terms. The Web site also serves as a means to communicate with the members of TAPS and chat with others. The TAPS website is located at: *http://www.the-atlantic-paranormal-society.com/index.html*

There are now countless organizations that study or "hunt" the paranormal. Thanks to the Internet, you can likely find one that covers your geographic area. Mediums and psychics also found popularity through the Internet and are a lot easier to find now.

If you're grieving over a lost loved one, contact a medium. If you're grieving over a dog, cat or other pet, a medium or a specialist in the art of Reiki can help you communicate with them to enhance emotional healing.

If you want to experience ghost walks or even ghost hunting, there are plenty of those groups and tours around, too. Just turn on your computer and surf the Internet.

CHAPTER 21
Conclusion

The interest people have in the paranormal ranges from a simple curiosity to a desire to reconnect with a loved one who has passed. Whether you are just seeking to prove if ghosts exist by hunting them in haunted locations, or seeking peace of mind by utilizing the talents of a medium to communicate with the deceased, it's important to remember that life exists beyond this world.

Energy cannot be destroyed, but it can be changed. The human soul (and the animal soul) is emotional energy, and our loved ones remain with us whenever we call to them, see a photograph of them or think about them. They come to us in our dreams (if they've passed into the light). They will be waiting for us when it is our time to pass, to welcome us into the next life. It is my experience that love never truly dies, and it even transcends from the afterlife to this life. Just keep an open mind, watch for signs and have faith.

If you think you may have mediumistic abilities, explore your family tree and see if any relatives have been known to communicate with ghosts and spirits. Then you can learn how to meditate and channel them.

Learn as much as you can, and in the words of medium Suzane Northrop, "practice, practice, practice" your abilities, and trust in the messages you receive.

My abilities sharpened when I fell in love and my emotions heightened. Emotion acts as an energizer for spirits and ghosts to transmit their messages. Remember that ghosts and spirits need energy, whether it is emotional or physical energy like electricity or moving water.

If you get messages from someone who has passed, some will be difficult to figure out. It doesn't mean what you're getting is wrong. It just means that spirits are showing you something that makes sense to them, but may not make sense to you or the person they're trying to communicate with. Sometimes, too, the person to whom the message is intended won't immediately understand the significance of what a medium has been shown.

For example, an elderly woman named Anna that came to me (after she passed) showed me farms and fields like the ones I saw in Minnesota when I visited there. It turned out she resided in a retirement home that faced an agricultural field in Maryland. But, she showed me a vision that would tell me there was a field near her home when she was alive. So, keep asking questions to those you are trying to convey messages to, so they can see how a message from beyond may apply to them. Meanwhile, read all of the references you can, and practice, practice, practice.

To follow along on my latest adventures or share your adventures or questions, visit our blog at:

http://ghostsandspiritsinsights.blogspot.com/.

You can also email me at *Rgutro@gmail.com.*

BIBLIOGRAPHY

CHAPTER 1: Growing Up and Developing an Understanding
Mechanics of Heat
*http://coolcosmos.ipac.caltech.edu//cosmic_classroom/light_lessons/th
ermal/heat.html*
Talking to Heaven, by James Van Praagh, 1997, Dutton Signet Book.
Ghosts Among Us, by James Van Praagh, 2008, Harper Collins.
When Ghosts Speak, by Mary Ann Winkowski, 2007, Grand Central
Publishing.

CHAPTER 4: Where Do Ghosts And Spirits Appear?
Wikipedia, Definition of "Apports":
http://en.wikipedia.org/wiki/Apport
Includes References
http://parapsych.org/historical_terms.html Historical Terms Glossary
of the Parapsychological Association, entry on Apport, Retrieved Sept
6, 2007
Fontana, David (2005). *Is There an Afterlife: A Comprehensive Review
of the Evidence*. Hants, UK: O Books, 352-381. ISBN 1903816904.
Kentucky Paranormal Research – Definition of "apport."
CHAPTER 6: How Can People Experience Ghosts?
Lisa Williams Medium and Clairvoyant,
www.lisawilliamsmedium.com
Talking to Heaven, by James Van Praagh, 1997, Dutton Signet Book.
Heaven and Earth, by James Van Praagh, 2001, Pocket Books.
Ghosts Among Us, by James Van Praagh, 2008, Harper Collins.
When Ghosts Speak, by Mary Ann Winkowski, 2007, Grand Central
Publishing.
EVP: http://en.wikipedia.org/wiki/Electronic_voice_phenomenon.
How Dogs Think, by Stanley Coren, p. 40, 2004, Simon and Schuster,
Inc.

CHAPTER 8: My Life Among Ghosts And Spirits
An Inherited Ability?
We Are Their Heaven, by Allison DuBois, 2006, Fireside Books,
Simon and Schuster.

CHAPTER 15: Experiences in Various Houses and Locations
SOURCE: *http://www.tombstoneaz.net/birdcage.php3*
SOURCE FOR FATIMA: *http://www.ghost-trackers.org/birdcage.htm*

The Complete Book of Ghosts by Paul Roland, 2007, Chartwell Books, Arcturus Publishing Limited.

CHAPTER 16: Ghost Walks in Various Cities:
Annapolis: The William Paca House: Beverly Litsinger, Maryland Ghost and Spirit Association, *www.marylandghosts.com/*
Ourgeorgiahistory.com
Savannah Hauntings, by Robert Edgerly, 2005, See Savannah Books, pp. 8
Visit-historic-savannah.com

CHAPTER 17: Dogs and Cats Do Go To Heaven: My Dog Buzz-Wyatt's Presence
Craig's 365 Blog: *http://craig365photo.blogspot.com*
How Dogs Think, by Stanley Cowen, pp. 74, 2004, Simon and Schuster, Inc.
Talking to Heaven, by James Van Praagh, p. 135, 1997, Penguin Putnam.

Janiceervin.com, Seminar: "A Closer Look: After Death Communications" in Chantilly, Virginia, on May 2, 2009, with medium Barbara Mallon.

Article: "Good deeds: Readers give thanks Neighbors come to aid after puppy killed" *Annapolis Capital* on March 13, 2005, Rob Gutro, *http://www.hometownannapolis.com/cgi-bin/read/2005/03_13-71/TOP*.

Reiki.org – What is Reiki – a Brief Overview:
http://www.reiki.org/FAQ/FAQHomepage.html

Reiki Instructor Email, permission granted by Fay, the Reiki instructor in Maryland. Fay can still be reached at *REIKISPEAK@aol.com* for anyone interested in the art of Reiki, or anyone who wants to communicate with a beloved pet that may have passed.

CHAPTER 19: PART TWO: Ghost / Spirit Stories From Others
Jennifer N. from MD is: Jennifer Nesbitt <z11nn11a@yahoo.com>

CHAPTER 20: Brief History of the Spiritual Movement
Psychics and Medium Network, UK: The Official Website Of The Psychic Mediums Craig & Jane Hamilton-Parker
http://www.psychics.co.uk/

TAPS *http://www.the-atlantic-paranormal-society.com/index.html*
Wikipedia: *http://en.wikipedia.org/wiki/Theosophical_Society*
http://www.s-upton.com/spm/history.htm

ABOUT THE AUTHOR

Rob considers himself an average guy, who just happens to be able to hear, feel, sense and communicate with Earth-bound ghosts and spirits who have passed on.

He enjoys talking about weather, especially hurricanes. He speaks at schools, museums, and social organizations about weather.

Rob worked as a radio broadcast meteorologist at the Weather Channel and was heard providing forecasts on more than 40 radio stations across the U.S. He worked for various other science-related organizations and has almost 20 years of on-air radio broadcasting experience.

Rob enjoys spending time with his partner and their two dogs. He enjoys taking ghost walks in various cities and visiting historic houses and sites to see who is still lingering behind and encourages them to move into the light to find peace.

He loves to exercise, enjoys a good cup of coffee, paperback mysteries, talking about ghosts and spirits, weather, superheroes and still reads and collects comic books. In fact, since he was a boy, one of his favorite superheroes has always been the ghostly avenger created in the 1940s called "The Spectre."

CPSIA information can be obtained at www.ICGtesting.com
Printed in the USA
BVOW031125181211

278641BV00007B/25/P